Harry S. Broudy, Professor of Education at
versity of Illinois, has taught at Massachuse
Colleges in North Adams and Framingham
been a visiting lecturer in philosophy and
tion at Boston University, New York Uni
the University of Southern California, ar
University of Florida. He is the author of *Bu*
a Philosophy of Education and co-author
Eugene L. Freel of *Psychology for General E*
tion. Dr. Broudy is a frequent contributor to
books and professional journals and is a past p
dent of the Association for Realistic Philosophy
Philosophy of Education Society.

Paradox and Promise

HARRY S. BROUDY

Paradox and Promise

Essays on American Life
and Education

1961

Prentice-Hall, Inc.

Englewood Cliffs, N. J.

LIBRARY OF CONGRESS
CATALOG CARD NO.: 61-14152

PRINTED IN THE UNITED STATES OF AMERICA

64852-C

Preface

There is no dearth of learned treatises about education and no lack of urbane wisdom about life in our time. There are many serious and even angry books about the American public schools and colleges. If there is any excuse for adding another item to the inventory, it is that education and life are so complex that different perspectives are easily come by, and each new one discloses items hitherto unnoticed, some of which are of more than passing interest.

The perspectives from which these essays have been written range through those of teachers, educational administrators, devotees of the liberal arts, educationists, would-be philosophers, and thoughtful human beings who want to reap the material benefits of technology without sacrificing the fruits of the human spirit.

The variety of perspectives may help to explain and, I hope, to justify to some degree the differences of mood found in these essays. If some themes seem to be treated less solemnly than they deserve, I can only plead that for a given purpose and in a given perspective their comic aspects are more noticeable and significant than their serious ones.

These essays owe so much to so many students and colleagues than any attempt to acknowledge the debt would leave most of my creditors unpaid; however, I am especially grateful to Dr. and Mrs. Joe Burnett for a helpful reading of the manuscript and to Edgar P. Thomas of Prentice-Hall, Inc., for his interest in the project as a whole.

University of Illinois
1961

H. S. B.

Table of Contents

Paradoxes in School & Society

Tales In & Out of School

Paradox & Promise

Paradox and Promise

Paradoxes in School & Society

Some Educational Paradoxes

Although it would be officially denied, Russia must have a ministry devoted exclusively to upsetting Americans, and inasmuch as we are upset by nearly everything the Russians do, it must be concluded that this ministry is unusually successful.

When the minister who had charge of upsetting Americans in the fall of 1957 regales his grandchildren with his exploits, *L'affaire* Sputnik will be near the top of his list. That orbiting a satellite would infect us with rocket fever could have been expected, but the controversy about public schools that it set off came as a surprise.

This controversy has had several distinctive features. For one thing, education is rarely perceived as being directly involved in national survival. In the Sputnik excitement it was so perceived. The searching out of laggard schoolmen was no less keen than the corresponding hunt for laggard scientists and generals. For school people this was heady stuff.

For another thing, the controversy made Americans so conscious of Russian education that the study of it became a thriving enterprise. I am told that educational exploration of the Russians is now on the wane and that the next continent listed for invasion by our cultural commandos is Africa. This is all to the good for reasons too obvious to mention.

Another feature gives the controversy an eerie strangeness. It is that each side keeps repeating its charges, completely indifferent to the arguments of the other side. It is, therefore, a kind of neurotic controversy—in which the participants are curiously unimpressed by reality.

Leaving aside individual variations in name calling and derision, we note that the controversy is primarily between those who want to "restore" the schools to the curriculum, methods, and virtues of some previous and presumably better day and those schoolmen who bravely insist that the changes in the American public school effected in the last twenty-five years are justified by the changes in the social scene. Let us call the former the "restorers" and the latter the "adapters."

The "restorers" want to return to hard subjects and hard study under a firm no-nonsense set of teachers and principles. Science, mathematics, languages, history, literature, and other disciplines commonly found in the repertory of the liberal arts college are to make up the curriculum. They want high school students to read fluently, speak and write precisely, and *know* the fundamentals of the subjects they are to study in college. Furthermore, they want the bright youngsters to buckle down and stop loafing.

The "restorers" point to certain independent secondary schools as shining examples of what can be done with American youth if a firm hand and a firm curriculum are combined. People had been saying this sort of thing for a long time, especially since the outbreak of World War II, but aside from a few books that caught the public fancy such as Arthur E. Bestor's *Educational Wastelands,* Albert Lynd's *Quackery in the Public Schools,* and Mortimer Smith's *And Madly Teach* these protests were heeded by small audiences.

The "adapters" dismissed these protests as the dyspeptic rumbles of reactionaries and conservatives nostalgic for the kind of schools in which the upper classes had been nurtured for centuries. With the ascension of Sputnik, however, the "restorers'" criticism overnight acquired powerful allies, especially in the daily press and in certain large circulation magazines such as *Life* and *Time.*

The military, best represented by the uninhibited remarks of Admiral Hyman G. Rickover, took up the cry that the "new" education had left us behind in the race for bigger and more powerful rockets and missiles. Having pioneered the first nuclear submarine, the Admiral, so to speak, achieved educational depth by association.

As the chorus of complaints grew louder it was clear that it was a chorus of mixed voices. College professors, for example, got the feeling of being needed to save the Nation instead of being accused of betraying it to the Left. For years they had complained bitterly that their students could not write, speak, or think at a level seemly for advanced work in their subjects. Remedial reading and writing classes had sprung up on college campuses on the theory that what college students lack, the colleges ought to provide. Instead of being shouted down as intellectual snobs, these professors now came into their innings and they stepped up to the plate and swung for the circuit. Or to preserve the metaphor, they lustily joined the chorus.

The professors were quite justified in their complaints, but they were also embarrassed by a small dilemma. They could not enjoy the benefits of huge post-Sputnik enrollments and at the same time demand that the new hordes of college students speak, write, and think with a degree of precision that only a small proportion of the school population had ever acquired. So they grumbled loudly but, on the whole, ineffectively; when the chips were down they preferred to earn a good salary teaching indifferently prepared students than to eke out a meager living consorting with only first-rate ones.

Perhaps to shift the guilt resulting from this moral suppleness, certain liberal arts professors needed a scapegoat. On the university campus they found one. The school or college of education was prospering by virtue of the fact that teachers were required to take courses in education or to earn degrees in education in order to be certified and to secure salary increments. Inasmuch as the professors had themselves become top-flight teachers without benefit of education courses, it was clear to them that the courses and degrees purveyed by the colleges of education were at best useless and at worst a fraud perpetrated on teachers and the public by the "educationists."

The intellectual competence of the professors of education and of their students accordingly came in for scorn and derision; their courses were ridiculed and certification laws brought under sharp attack. Einstein, it was jeeringly pointed out, could not have been certified to teach mathematics in New York or Illinois high schools. This was presumably the clincher, although why anyone would want to have Einstein teaching high school mathematics is itself a puzzle. Faculty wives with A.B. degrees from good colleges found themselves prevented from teaching their major subjects in local high schools without first taking courses in "education." This infuriated them, and their husbands even more.

In the post-Sputnik era the "restorers" received a mighty assist from the grey-flannel-suit contingent in the community. Graduates of liberal arts colleges, they had made their way up in their organizations and now wanted the kind of secondary school that would prepare their sons and daughters for entrance into a *good* college. They were bitter about their local high school if it did not do so. Their bitterness was unusually keen if they could not quite afford to ship their offspring to the more expensive private preparatory schools. But even if they could and did, the mounting cost of the public schools made them victims of taxation without benefit, at least as far as their own children were concerned.

Not least effective in the chorus of protest were tax haters of all kinds. They were convinced somehow that the traditional type of schooling would be cheaper than the "new" kind.

In the ensemble were also to be found advocates of parochial or religious schooling. Regarding the public school as godless and materialistic, they found themselves consorting with a strange variety of humanists and anticlericals in urging restoration of the old educational order.

The combined outburst found the "adapters" outgunned theoretically and practically. In the Thirties the Progressive schoolmen (a species of the genus "adapters") had gone on the offensive. The leaders of our industrial empire were cutting sorry figures, a new social order was long overdue, and with the help of the New Deal it was on the way to being installed. The depression and the political temper of the times put the liberals in a strong position to democratize the American school and to throw its weight behind the liberal movements of the day.

Theoretically, the new education really had only two big guns. One was that a greater proportion of the population stayed in school for longer periods of time. The other was that this large secondary school population did not need the older type of college preparatory curriculum and probably did not have the academic aptitudes to master it anyway. After all, most of these youngsters would neither enter the learned professions nor sit in the seats of the managers. Ancient history, language, and mathematics, it was argued, could contribute nothing but headaches to "non-academic youth" in earning a living or living with other people in a democratic community.

The life-adjustment curriculum, accordingly, found its way into the thinking of the "adapters." Mental health, vocational preparation, preparation for family and community living seemed to be what the average citizen needed and only prejudiced reactionaries, they argued, held out for the traditional schooling. Only unenlightened parents eager for status and false prestige insisted that their children study Latin whether they needed it or not. A new social order meant new success routes and new values. Indeed, it called for a new type of man. In the school the new order meant a new way of learning for a new way of life. The "adapters" had a sense of mission, but like other missionaries they often encountered the greatest resistance in the ardor and sincerity of rival missionaries.

The debate was beclouded by the reluctance of both sides to be branded as undemocratic. One obvious solution, namely, subjects for the classes and life adjustment for the masses, smacked so much of elites, social cleavages, and snobbism, that even the conservatives dared not come out unequivocally for a two-track school system in which the masses and the classes say fond good-bye to each other at the end of the sixth grade, as indeed they do in Russia, England, France, and most of the continental countries.

A "restorer" like Robert Maynard Hutchins is likely to prescribe the class curriculum for the masses as well as the classes. This convinces nobody. Everyone concerned knows very well that, *as ordinarily taught,* the masses could not master the class curriculum even if one could demonstrate universal utility for it.

The "adapters," on the other hand, do not quite dare to continue business at the old stand. With Sputniks, and missiles, and astronauts about to take off for the moon, one cannot simply reiterate the requirements of ordinary decent citizenship as a design for American education. A democracy without intercontinental missiles and space men is not likely to remain democratic for long. "Adapters" have had to give in on special education for the gifted and unduly retarded children, while their opposition to "hard" subjects studied systematically without benefit of social motivation or sanctified by social needs has been considerably muted.

What neither side has fully understood is that we live in a time of paradox and contradiction and that such a time conspires to produce strange events, not only in outer space but in classrooms and PTA meetings as well.

Consider, for example, the Paradox of Difficulty and Ease. When in the history of the world has it been so difficult to understand the problems of citizenship? When has it been so hard to master the knowledge needed to understand such an ubiquitous problem as taxation? How many college graduates feel themselves competent to understand nuclear fission and the celestial mechanics involved in orbiting satellites? How many well-intentioned citizens would care to expound the intricacies of foreign affairs? The day when the average citizen reading his local newspaper and conversing with his cronies at the general store could arrive at intelligent decisions about problems, foreign and domestic, is gone.

What has happened to the time when, to become a businessman, one saved $500 and opened a store? Or when one could read law for a while in some office and pass the bar? Or when a few years of schooling sufficed to turn out a general practitioner in medicine? In the learned professions the period of training has become longer, more theoretical, more abstract, more technical, more expensive, and more formidable to the aspirant with average intelligence and zeal.

In short, to be first rate at almost anything calls for more training, more self-discipline, more energy than ever before. Even the rearing of children, once taken in stride by mothers of five or six, has become an art with its own technique, theories, and mystique. Writing advice to mothers, young and aged, is a major industry. Dr. Spock's book on baby care has usurped the place once held by the family Bible; it is regarded with no less reverence and consulted with far greater frequency.

Is it any wonder that many people who have tried to become first-rate at their profession, or at anything else, for that matter, are depressed—indeed almost overwhelmed—by the need for so much knowledge, training, and self-discipline? And is it surprising that they scold the schools for not being equally concerned for first-rateness?

It is quite natural, therefore, for the status-seekers, for the men with ambition, for the leaders or would-be leaders of the community to range themselves in the educational debate on the side of hard, theoretical, and intellectual subjects, and on those traits of character that will propel the student through these subjects even when he would prefer to be out fishing.

The attitude of these people reflects the fact that the technological paradise, like its theological prototype, has at its center the tree of knowledge: knowledge of specialists, by specialists, and for specialists. These specialists include not only the members of the professions, high-level technicians, and managers in every enterprise from the running of supermarkets to armies, but also those who seek, formulate, and teach the knowledge needed by these specialists, that is to say, the professors in particular, and the intellectuals in general.

Let us now inspect the social scene through another pair of eyes. Imagine a young man in high school asking himself one fine morning what he wants out of life and what he needs to do to get it. First, he wants money, but how much and for what? For an automobile, obviously, and an impressive array of other material goods that most men do, as a matter of course, possess. As he thinks ahead beyond his stint of military service, he foresees himself married to one of his pretty classmates, living in a small but modern house equipped to the eaves with mechanical appliances. They will be blessed with plenty of leisure for fun and frolics, and with a modest brood of children who are to be launched in a similar, albeit perhaps even more comfortable, orbit.

How does one get these blessings? By taking a job in one of the factories or business establishments. What kind of job? On the assembly line, in delivery, on various levels of clerking and selling, packing, checking, loading, and in a thousand and one other operations for which men are needed in the complex working of modern industry.

How much schooling does one need for this kind of work? How well, for example, does one have to speak or write? As to speaking, no better than if one never went to school at all and never so well as to offend one's job mates. As to writing, one should be able to fill out forms, sign papers, write simple letters to mail order houses, parents, and spouses. While women occasionally write letters to friends, the average man either telephones his friends or waits until he runs into them. Is it an exaggeration to say that the vocational requirements of the vast majority of jobs do not call for a development in language usage any higher than that achieved by the end of junior high school?

Take mathematics. Each vocation has its own needs, to be sure, but most of our occupations rarely require anything more abstruse than simple arithmetic. Machines now perform most of the computation needed in business establishments, and the needs of domestic calculations are not great. Even at somewhat higher levels, mathematical computations can be reduced to mechanical routines or the use of handbooks and formulas, so that the amount and quality of mathematical thinking remains within the limits of people with moderate intelligence and an elementary school education.

Literature, history, foreign language, art? Does our adolescent really need much mastery of these disciplines for the kind of life he is dreaming about? Will his neighbors, working mates, and friends look down on him if he should be ignorant in these matters? Or are they more likely to be suspicious of undue sophistication? After all, with a television set, a radio, illustrated magazines, and digests of all varieties, does one need to break one's back, so to speak, to become unduly proficient in scholastic skills?

The candid answer must be "no." Here is an image of the good life in America that requires little in the way of knowledge, skill, and strength. Just as the modern automobile requires little automotive knowledge on the part of the driver and much automotive knowledge from its designer, so our whole technological civilization has made the knowledge underlying and supporting it indispensable for a few but easily dispensable for the many. To paraphrase Winston Churchill, never have so many lived so well on the brains of so few.

On many occasions, however, the parents of the adolescent who is so obligingly serving as an illustration for our argument may not be happy with their son's modest dreams for the future. The life he envisions, they may admit, is not bad; certainly it is neither uncomfortable nor useless. Could not the son, however, aspire to the higher rungs of the social ladder? Could he not be the manager of the business instead of one of the clerks? An engineer instead of a laboratory technician? A physician instead of a hospital attendant? And would these questions not become peculiarly poignant if the boy had a high order of intelligence or, to be less hereditarian, a high scholastic aptitude?

The adolescent might well summon to his defence authorities both ancient and contemporary. On the ancient side a long and powerful tradition warns that happiness does not lie along the paths of ambition and glory. The vanity of men has been discerned and decried in every epoch. Temporal power, high office, and personal glory, all of these are held to be transitory, fickle, and in the end disillusioning. Spinoza in both life and writings renounced them as goals. The psalmists; Marcus Aurelius, the Roman Emperor; Epictetus, the slave; Confucius, the Chinese sage; and Diogenes, the eccentric philosopher, all came to the same conclusion.

In our time the ulcer symbolizes the wages of worldly ambition. The high-powered executive, the ambition-ridden man, the overcommitted man, the anxiety-soaked man, and the status-hungry man are doomed to ulcers of the body or the spirit or both. The neurotic ones, the mixed-up ones, the angry ones are types already familiar to the adolescent. He is, he feels, no Brain, no Eager Beaver, no Alger hero. He is willing to settle for what he can reasonably expect to have, and by all standards this is pretty good indeed.

Is it then so surprising that many men and women believe that the skills of social adjustment, of living with others, of living in communities, of doing one's civic and domestic chores cheerfully and democratically are far more important than a rat race to the top of the organization ladder? Is not this the new wisdom? Is not our adolescent a modern sage?

And if we are of a like mind, shall we not ask the school to help the young acquire these skills and attitudes rather than to put them through intellectual paces for a rat race they have renounced? Naturally, parents want their children to be both learned and happy, but if they must choose, how many will not sacrifice learning for happiness? A's in mathematics do not compensate for being a wallflower and sitting beside a mute telephone.

It is further understandable that within the camp of educators, there will be theorists who argue persuasively for a school system that would meet these attitudes halfway. The life-adjustment curriculum is the educational expression of this attitude. While its proponents may themselves harbor ulcers and be neurotically driven to power and distinction, this does not in the least affect the truth of the theory itself: that for the common American man the intensive study of hard subjects is neither necessary nor even desirable.

Instead, educators of this persuasion aim rather to inculcate strong attitudes about democratic ways of thinking and doing. And this necessarily means playing down invidious comparisons. Inequalities of capacity are to be interpreted as due to inequalities of opportunity and not to heredity. Differences in vocations are to be regarded as merely different ways of being socially useful, so that the engineer and the ditchdigger are equally valuable because both contribute to the social good. Highbrows in every area are to be given their come-uppance. Class distinctions are to be deplored and abolished as soon as possible. Economic, social, and political democracy are the triple goals of social reform, and to arouse enthusiasm for the crusade is the first business of the school.

That this view of the American public school owes its theoretical underpinning to John Dewey is undeniable. In his writings the thrust is always against the philosophical and social tradition of the West, insofar as they defended class distinctions or any distinctions among and within individuals that would impede sharing and community. Dewey believed that science offered the best hope that the sharing could be a rational and intelligent civic process.

The fear and desperation of the Thirties gave urgency to the need for social and economic reform. It marked the climax of the so-called "reconstructionist" mission to make the school an instrument of social reform via social and political action, a mission powered by a faith that the school in twelve years could form attitudes strong enough to produce political and social effects shortly thereafter.

Events in the Forties and Fifties took much of the steam out of the Progressive school movement precisely because they demonstrated that in times of crisis a technological civilization cannot survive without a large and strong corps of theorists and technicians. Civic education, however sensible and valuable it might be for reconstructing the social order, could not be relied upon to save it in wars hot or cold, if it did not produce the scientists to win the missile race.

There is, however, a profound difference between the zeal of a Progressive educator for the welfare of the common man and the good-humored modesty of our adolescent's plan to be one. Our "hero" is as much amused by the Progressives' call to social reform as he is by the frenzy of Madison Avenue. For the Progressive schoolman is no less an advocate of the strenuous life than is the man in the grey flannel suit; they differ only in the activities in which they propose to be strenuous.

Our young man, however, is against the strenuous life altogether and prefers to operate on the rational and natural principle of least effort. It would be less than rational not to take advantage of the exertions of a few hard-working brains when the whole technological enterprise would go bang if we did not consume the goods it produced. Our young hero differs moreover from the sages of antiquity who also counseled moderation of desire and ambition. They substituted the cultivation of one's spiritual powers, a task that was no less strenuous but which they believed to be more rewarding than striving for earthly glory and power. To our hero, this mood together with the social zeal of the "adapters" and the intellectual zeal of the elite are all equally "square." One humorous aspect, therefore, about the educational controversy is that the bulk of its proposed beneficiaries reject their would-be benefactors in both camps.

Not so humorous is the possibility that the debate over the kind of schooling we need to save ourselves is a surface symptom, the result of a more fundamental contradiction in the requirements of modern life. Until we understand this and find some way to make peace with it or to overcome it, we are destined to have many debates that apparently get nowhere. On the other hand, it is just possible that not every contradiction is real; perhaps some are only apparent.

What are some of these contradictions? Let us list a few of them, and leave it to subsequent essays to discuss some of them in detail.

One of these paradoxes has already been touched on: Never has it been so difficult for a man to be first-rate, and never has it been so easy to be second-rate, and never has being second-rate been so comfortable.

Another is that the more democratic our social order becomes, i.e., the more widely our people share in the benefits of a technological society, the more indispensable does an intellectual and technological elite become, yet—can a nation remain democratic if it is controlled by elites?

Another is that the more we satisfy our material wants by reaping the fruits of modern industry, the harder it is to squeeze spiritual satisfaction from it.

Still another is that the more secular life becomes the more a priesthood of diverse specialists is needed to intercede for us with (to the layman) the mysterious workings of medicine, law, business, finance, and automobile mechanics. More and more it becomes obvious that all of us must belong to some occupational specialty and be at the mercy of every other specialty.

Yet so rich are the possibilities of American life that for nearly every individual there is a choice among the levels at which he can live, ranging from the absurdly easy to the painfully difficult.

We can, by cajoling, threatening, and appealing, persuade a man to undertake strenuous training for this or that specialty and conceivably we could in time make of every man a first-rate performer in some endeavor. But that large numbers of men will undertake to make first-rate human beings of themselves seems unlikely, especially when the second- and third-rate states of human existence are so rewarding.

And yet unless all citizens are to become first-rate *persons,* the school system will inevitably sort out the students into elites and masses. Or better, the students themselves will split the system up and whether different curricula are housed in one or many buildings will not make much difference.

This will be a multi-track school system, however, and that is precisely what the American dream did not dream about. If we cannot give up the hard subjects and the hard discipline that elites require, and if we cannot sell them to all on the basis that every person needs them in his work, then our only recourse is to argue that every one needs them as a person, but only if one decides to be a first-rate person.

This is the great virtue of the logically-organized subjects developed in Western civilization. They are not only prerequisite for maintaining a technological social order, but taken together they are necessary *today* for being a first-rate citizen and person. They are thus the natural material of common education for first-rate living.

The difficulty with the life-adjustment pattern for common education is precisely that although it gives all citizens admirable attitudes and a kind of common understanding about the ways of the community and the world, it is hard put to supply the systematic knowledge of the sciences, history, literature, and philosophy that first-rate citizenship or technology entails.

It is by making the cultivated person our goal, rather than frenzied specialization, on the one hand, or amiable togetherness, on the other, that we can avoid the dangers of ulcers in the strenuous life. For the more strenuously one works to cultivate the self in all of its value potentialities, the more satisfying are both the process and the product. There is less fear, less insecurity, less need for aggression toward self and toward others. There is, in the words of psychologist Abraham Maslow, less energy devoted to overcoming real or imagined deficiencies and more to actualizing oneself in positive ways. Life changes from an escape to a journey of discovery, from reaction to action, from the dullness of the mediocre to the rewards of the peak experience. Such strenuousness does not produce ulcers.

That the American public will be charmed by the prospect of strenuous self-cultivation seems unlikely. For one thing, self-cultivation is difficult to publicize. Those who dedicate themselves to the enterprise of becoming first-rate human beings are not highly visible. They are not suitable subjects for success stories but neither is their example horrible enough to warrant special articles with pictures in the large circulation magazines. It is only when self-cultivation is associated with great wealth or championship performance in boxing or banking that it is regarded as newsworthy. Ordinary instances of self-cultivation do not acquire enough status to serve as models for the young. Yet such are precisely the models our children need, and the lack of them lames the educative process because one seductive example is worth a thousand homilies.

There is a solution. There always is, but this one is so fantastic that one hestitates to advance it even in half seriousness. It is that the teachers themselves become the models of the good life. Teachers have this advantage: they are already accustomed to anonymity and they are already models of a sort.

Unfortunately, our culture does not cast them in this role. Models of circumspectness, thrift, and propriety they are expected to be, but not of self-cultivation. Leisure, study, serenity, frequent association with books and the arts, not to speak of the other dimensions of excellence, are requisites of self-cultivation, and these come high in our economy. The sort of people who cherish and cultivate these values are not likely to be found in large numbers in the classrooms of the American public schools.

Yet they *could be* found there and may yet be. Not because of any causes that one can now foresee, but because events conspire to produce the least likely of consequences—and one can therefore pin one's hopes on one more paradox.

A Surfeit of Freedom

From many sources—social theorists, men of letters, philosophers, and theologians—comes the cry that modern man is losing his freedom and with it his peace of mind and integrity of soul.

Karl Mannheim, the eminent German social theorist, leaves us no alternative to a planned society. Our choice, he argues, is reduced to a society planned by totalitarian villains, emperors of industrial complexes, or by decent democratic citizens. Unfortunately, whoever makes the choice will also have to choose between rockets and butter; between mass-produced refrigerators or no refrigerators at all for masses of people. In other words, societies that commit themselves to acquiring the blessings of mass production do not have much choice as to the means of achieving them. Large-scale machine industry by its own logic makes certain demands on materials, institutions, and human beings; it is no respector of ideologies.

From the poets and novelists come jeers at modern man's pretensions to freedom. The post-war writings paint us as puppets in the hands of angry gods; wisps of straw in the gale of events. War, peace, peaceful war, warlike peace—which of us as an individual chooses among these? Probably nobody. The intellectual and the artist resent not being consulted in these matters and rage appropriately. The common man now as in every age does not rage; he just grumbles at something he cannot name and assuredly cannot understand.

Neo-orthodox theologians such as Niebuhr, Barth, and Tillich have grimly smitten us hip and thigh. Events have proved, they believe, that the pride of the Enlightenment in the self-sufficiency of man in the shaping of his destiny and salvation has been rebuked. We need help from on High, and the only real freedom we have is to acknowledge the need and source of such help. Social science has not conquered original sin, and social service has not given us spiritual adjustment.

Through the influence of an interesting coalition of Continental Existentialists and American psychoanalysts, it is becoming fashionable to blame the anxieties of our time, the loss of identity and the resultant search for it, escapism, strong guilt feelings, and powerful urges to aggression upon the lack of individual freedom consequent upon the exigencies of modern life in a social order dominated by the demands of large-scale industry. Either we agree with Jean-Paul Sartre that it makes no rational sense to believe man is free and therefore the only thing to do is to assert it anyway; or we believe with Erich Fromm that having freedom is more disturbing than not having it.

The agitation about man's freedom or the lack of it goes on, as it always has gone on, largely in the mind of intellectuals. The common man, assumes the intellectual, has little taste for soul-searching and is too thick-skinned and thick-tongued to feel or articulate the problems of modern man. The intellectuals are probably not quite right about this; but they are right in believing that it is their role to think and suffer ahead of their time. They are the sensitive free nerve endings of society.

Nevertheless, the intellectual is prone to overestimate the import of his own sensitivity. Until a disease penetrates to the inner depths of a vital organ, the organism is not in mortal danger and may not even feel pain. Until a social disorder makes itself felt in the life of the common man, it is not yet a full-blown social danger. Our world is a curious one precisely because so much of what in previous eras had been felt only by the cultivated few is now being experienced by the uncultivated multitudes. The joys and sorrows of freedom constitute a case in point.

Freedom is a disturbing element, a moral gadfly, wherever it appears; in its common every-day meanings as well as in the more subtle forms spun out by the dialectician. In other words, for any man to realize that he can relieve the misery of his neighbor is as disturbing (until he actually chooses to relieve it) as is the awareness for the religiously sensitive spirit that he is free to choose between eternal fire and eternal bliss.

It is of freedom in its ordinary meaning—the power to make our choices prevail—that we now have not a lack but a surfeit. The common man of today has more of this sort of freedom than had any nobleman of the Renaissance or king of antiquity, certainly more than he can comfortably manage.

What, for example, could Socrates, Alexander, Caesar, or the Medicis do about poverty, cancer, tuberculosis, heart disease, and a half-hundred other ills of man? About all the wisest and most powerful men of antiquity could do was to adopt an appropriate attitude toward them, namely, to regret and endure with fortitude what they could not cure. The Stoics were realists, not escapists.

Even Montaigne, the wisest of the Frenchmen, could do no more about his kidney stones than to adapt his life to them, just as he adapted himself to religious wars and the dangerous friendship of princes. Montaigne is perhaps an unusually illuminating representative of our theme, because he lived at a time when natural science was beginning to flex its muscles. He was, after all, a contemporary of Copernicus. Nevertheless, the technological possibilities of the natural sciences seem to have eluded him.

Montaigne had no more faith in medicine than he had in law—the two professions of which man might expect some help in his fight against the ills of the body and the body politic. He regarded both disciplines as bewildering, self-stultifying conglomerations of folk lore, lessons from experience, precedents, and prejudices. He made it a principle of his life to have as little to do with doctors and lawyers as he could, and he urged others to follow his example.

I take it that Montaigne's judgment about law is still popular. One still hears complaints about lawmakers that would not have surprised him. But about medicine Montaigne might have been wiser.

To be sure, even in our day Montaigne would derive small comfort from the medical men as far as his kidney stones were concerned. There is still no simple way of getting rid of them. However, could he have refused to undergo all the diagnostic procedures in which modern medicine is so rich? X-rays, tests, exploratory probings and operations, would Montaigne have refused to undertake them? Would he have been a moral coward if he had?

Not so long ago the common man suffering from kidney stones would have been forgiven if he had refused to undergo these diagnostic procedures. They are expensive and, as Socrates pointed out in the *Republic,* subtle diseases and cures are not for the working man. Today this is no longer an excuse even for the poorest among us. Indeed, the greater the poverty of the patient, the more likely it is that we have public means of paying his medical bills. The lowliest hobo has now been deprived of the moral luxury of letting nature take its course with him.

But the change is deeper than this. The plain, every-day American, with or without kidney stones, has a new power. He can contribute a dollar or more to some organization (there surely will be at least one) that is fostering research into the prevention and cure of kidney stones. By this donation or similar ones the individual makes possible the activation of massive organized research into the problems of heart disease, muscular dystrophy, mental illness, cancer, tuberculosis, arteriosclerosis, poverty, and ignorance. Neither the gold of Midas nor the wisdom and good will of Socrates and Montaigne could summon such power.

As to bearing nobly what must be endured, the common man cannot hold a candle to certain ancient heroes of the spirit. But he can give a dollar, and this represents real power and, consequently, freedom.

This power is fragmented among millions so that each individual portion thereof is by itself piddling, but we are no longer so naive as to belittle atoms because they are small. Tiny bits of profit, if there are enough of them, make millionaires. Tiny contributions collectively command the knowledge, skill, and effort needed to conquer evil. Montaigne had money to contribute but what agency in his culture could do anything with it?

Although modern man's individual power is small, the moral responsibility it imposes is not. Suppose I am confronted with the alternatives of contributing a dollar to the heart fund and spending it on two moderately priced alcoholic drinks. Is my responsibility greater if the sum is two dollars instead of one? How can we calculate responsibilities in such a situation? By the consequences? But who can imagine all the consequences of taking either alternative? By the quality of the decision I make as I choose one alternative and reject the other? But is not the moral quality of my experience in making a decision between two important alternatives always the same? There is, therefore, a sense in which moral responsibility is not divisible in the same way that power is, so the minuteness of the individual's power is not necessarily a sign that his moral task is minute.

With power then comes moral responsibility. About earthquakes I have no moral responsibility because there is nothing I can do about them —I cannot even contribute a dollar to an organization for the prevention of earthquakes. About victims of earthquakes, I can do something—send a dollar—and therefore I possibly have an obligation to do so. In any event, I have the duty to think about whether I should or not.

In the past man was spared much of this moral activity by ignorance.

We are told that the inaugurations of our presidents were delayed until March because it took so long to gather the results of the November elections from the remote corners of the country. About many earthquakes, sinkings at sea, famines, and even wars one did not hear for months or years. The import of rapid communications is that it deprives us of that most admirable of all moral exculpations—involuntary ignorance. Scarcely have the windows ceased to rattle, and the world knows that there has been an earthquake, how many victims will be homeless, and where to send the dollar to lessen their suffering.

As a matter of fact, even if a careful reading of newspapers does not apprise us of disasters, we can be sure they are befalling our fellow men somewhere. The Red Cross in our time serves as a universal nonsectarian church for those who plan to secure salvation by good works. We can, consequently, make a donation to this organization at any time to atone for errors of commission, omission, and inadvertent ignorance. To sum it up, the average man has only a little power but almost no excuses for not using that little power in behalf of mankind.

Instead of the impotent, frustrated, organization-fettered man, I give you the common man with so great a potentiality for service to his fellows that he should be as morally sensitive as a candidate for clerical orders. The conditions for moral sensitivity are augmented by the opportunities afforded us to improve ourselves. Free schooling through the secondary school and beyond, free libraries beckoning accusingly, museums, concerts, records, and lectures galore make of every uneducated man a sinner guilty of sloth, frivolity, and fondness for the flesh pots.

Another condition commonly acknowledged as prerequisite for moral rectitude is to be selfless. So long as the ego is inflated, so long as pride rides high, there is little hope for moral regeneration. I submit that the moral situation described above entails a loss of self which like the freedom and power of the common man is literal and not figurative.

A dollar contributed to the good cause dissolves instantly into a sea of dollars. The identity of the donor lasts no longer than it takes to write out the receipt. There can be no question about the donor's motive. There can be no social approval for his deed, and the chances that some journalist will celebrate his obscurity are so small as to be discounted in calculating his moral merit. Anonymity insures his purity of heart.

I am sure that this elevation of our common man to moral heroism will strike the reader as a burlesque of the moral drama. It will be objected that merely giving dollars to this and that good cause robs the moral drama of its urgency, its doubts, and its agonizing search of the soul. Moral depth demands that we be overwhelmed by the moral imperative and that we validate the majesty of humanity by being overwhelmed.

As a dramatic spectacle it must be conceded that the moral efforts of the common man are not impressive. As a protagonist the common man is so feeble compared to the institutions, systems, and forces of which he is such a little part, that whatever he does has difficulty in being interesting, not to say, significant. Placed alongside of the great battle against cancer or heart disease, the donation of a dollar is miniscule. The little man and his moral battle is not unlike the infantryman who shoots his rifle in the general direction of the enemy. The damage he inflicts is problematical; the damage he receives is individual and real.

Such drama, as the donation of the dollar and the bullets of the infantryman do have, must be sought *within* the person, not in the external appearance of his act. On big stages or little ones the drama of the situation is intensified as the opportunity for critical choices increases.

Have we fully used our opportunities to improve ourselves and others? The availability of these opportunities to the common man now places upon him a moral burden heretofore reserved for the rich and the fortunate.

Have we learned enough to bring up our children properly? At one time the common man could have excused himself from such sophistication. Today free lectures, articles in low-priced magazines, adult education courses, and all sorts of pamphlets create a duty for every parent.

Have we had sufficient check-ups to catch serious ailments in time? The man with an incurable disease has always symbolized the tragic. It was a situation that could be turned to moral and dramatic account; it was a stern test of a man's character.

What happens, however, when an incurable disease by advance in knowledge becomes curable, but only if caught in time? Quiet resignation to and bold defiance of early death no longer are regarded as heroic. These attitudes are either idiotic or morally bad. As far as the family is concerned, they are the height of selfishness. At a stroke, the duty to submit to frequent checkups looms large. Consider in this connection the moral struggles imposed on the smoker, drinker, and eater by scientific pronouncements on what overindulgence may cause. No St.

Anthony emerges from these quietly desperate struggles between the lusts of the flesh and the fear of cancer, heart disease, diabetes, and a host of other ailments. Nevertheless, the struggles are real and painful.

There is no lack of drama but the dramatic impact is not upon the external observer. It is felt from the inside as doubt, indecision, anxiety, compulsion, and guilt; felt intensely, too, but one can hardly make a dramatic production out of getting or skipping a medical checkup.

To grasp the full significance of the moral drama as it is played out in the life of the common man requires imagination, or what Sören Kierkegaard and some others have called *inwardness*. It takes little inwardness for the Big Man to realize his role in the social drama, and it requires no more to face up to the fact that one has no role in it save that of a pawn. But it takes endless inwardness to grasp imaginatively how the real but minute contribution that the average man makes to world events shapes their total effect. It takes, in addition, a kind of simple faith to believe in oneself as an instrument of World purpose, Cosmic trend, or God—a kind of faith because it is based on feeble evidence.

The resemblance to the inwardness of the religious life can be carried further. A man whose whole life is centered in a concern for his eternal salvation does not announce to the world that his whole life is a concern for salvation. This is the kind of inwardness one does not externalize. Just how to carry off the religious life without falling into hypocrisy, smugness, pride, and selfishness is a problem that never ceased to puzzle Kierkegaard. He seemed to conclude that the truly religious inwardness can never be communicated directly by outward acts. Indirectly one can approximate it by not attracting attention to one's inner life, and this can be accomplished by living an ordinary, aesthetically insignificant, dramatically mediocre life and yet conveying the impression that one has a secret of great worth; not, of course, by announcing that one has a great secret, but rather by having the intensity of the inner life invest even ordinary life actions with a special significance.

Inwardness, unfortunately, is beset by two untoward circumstances. First, it has no obvious social value; it has no results in the world of events. In an age when everyone is striving for results, inwardness may acquire a subversive taint. Common men accomplishing little in the way of results but suspected of an intensive inner life may be haled into the courts.

A second and even more important deterrent is the tendency to regard inwardness as a sign of mental illness. These quiet ones; these withdrawn ones; these ambivalent ones are not adjusting well. An educational system committed to results and mental health will be suspicious of inwardness.

There are many signs betraying our distrust of inwardness, of the contemplative side of life, and of the aesthetic dimension of experience. Our educators and perhaps our clergymen as well are anxious to be mistaken for men of business, astronauts, generals, and social engineers. These are not good omens for cultivation of inwardness in the young.

Psychiatrists are quite right in shaking their heads at the overly timid, self-preoccupied, withdrawn child, if in his withdrawal he escapes from reality into a fantasy world. This is what A. H. Maslow has called D-cognition or the kind of mental activity concerned primarily with repairing our lacks and inadequacies. But true inwardness is not deficiency repair. It is more like Maslow's B-cognition (Being Cognition) in which men can see more clearly than usual how things really are in themselves rather than merely noting their power to serve us.

And it is precisely this clarity of understanding that the modern man must have about his freedom and his power, his minuteness and his greatness, or he will truly go crazy. For what can drive us insane more surely and more quickly than vacillating between a belief that it is of utmost importance to make decisions and the equally strong belief that nothing we do really makes any difference in the vast currents of our time?

It is not true, therefore, that modern man, the common man of our time, is suffering from a lack of genuine freedom. If anything, his troubles are occasioned by a surfeit of freedom and the responsibility for decision that goes with freedom.

What is true is that the common man is no more ready for this new power and new freedom than he is for the new leisure. It is no wonder, therefore, that he tries to flee from it. It is far easier to leave freedom to Fate or the Great and to use freedom to complain against both of them.

To live in the intermediate state—between iron necessity and a modicum of power—calls for a cultivated mind, a lively imagination, and a sense of humor. When formal education recognizes the nature of modern man's freedom, it will perspire less freely in trying to make him believe that he has great political, social, or economic power. It will then be freer to cultivate the citizen's mind, his imagination, and his sense of humor. It takes all of these to gaze steadily on the spectacle of grown men in frock coats playing games at conference tables, and great minds, perhaps our greatest, working relentlessly to send heaps of metal to the moon before someone else does.

For if one concentrates on this spectacle inwardly on its minutest details and from all sides, the moment will come when one begins to laugh. But the point is never to laugh out loud, for the sober truth is that it is no laughing matter. These eager, busy, and intelligent beavers can destroy themselves and the spectators too. They very well may do just that, for they are at bottom a humorless lot.

It takes cultivation, imagination, and a sense of humor to nurse one's own little spark of power and freedom—those little dollars that one can donate to causes great and small as if these dollars were really great and important. It is best to display the gravity that little children assume when adults think they are playing. Children know better. They know they are not playing at all, but if the adults think so, all the better.

The Burden of Leisure

Thoughtful people, especially the solemn ones, announce impending crises of civilization so frequently that after a while we cease to be alarmed. Accordingly, whenever the disaster does occur, most of us, despite the numerous warnings, are caught unprepared. The solemn ones have all the arguments on their side, but just as we never learn to heed their warnings, so they never seem to learn that we are not going to.

It is only with moderate solemnity, therefore, that we ought to announce the crisis which the new leisure portends for our culture within the next decade, and we thoughtful ones ought not to repeat the announcement indiscriminately from every housetop.

That we are on the verge of receiving extraordinary increments of leisure is attested by the following circumstances. First is the rate at which automation is taking over the control of machines in industry, retail merchandising, and in the clerical services. We once thought that non-intelligent machines had to be supervised by intelligent workers. Now we know that the way to supervise non-intelligent machines is by setting other non-intelligent machines to stand guard over their divagations.

If we wish to keep a room at a temperature of 70 degrees, we set a thermostat to shut the burner off when the mercury in the thermometer reaches the 70-degree mark, and to put it back into motion when the room cools to below 70. Few household thermostats can manage this. Instead, they kick on at around 68 degrees and kick off at around 72. This is good enough for most of us most of the time, but if it were not we could, I suppose, devise an electric eye arrangement that would be so sensitive to the movement of the mercury column that it could kick the thermostat into action at 69.99 degrees and kick it off at 70.01 degrees. Even this degree of accuracy seems pretty crude compared to what electronic controls are capable of achieving under laboratory conditions.

We are not yet sure at what point an intelligent creature is indispensable to the process of having one non-intelligent machine control the errors of another. In any event, a lot of machine watchers in days to come will have to watch machines operating at a higher level of sensitivity than those they watched before, and this may reduce the number of watchers needed or the hours they watch. One way or another, we Americans are going to work so few hours to produce a spectacular plenitude of goods and services that we shall make a laughing stock out of the Communists and the Pessimists. We shall out-eat everybody, out-live everybody, out-enjoy everybody, out-comfort everybody, and all in a handful of working hours per week per man.

So much for the typical middle-aged worker. A thirty-hour week distributed over five days a week for eleven months of the year seems a not unreasonable schedule to envision for the bulk of the working force. I see no reason for making an exception in the case of professional workers, as some are wont to do. Automation can reduce the number of persons and hours needed in the service occupations as well as in the manufacturing ones. Barbers already are using mechanical clippers and blowers and could utilize recordings and earphones to supply their customers' needs for conversation. Electronically controlled hair clipping machines are not beyond possibility. Doctors, lawyers, and college professors likewise can cut down the hours they spend on gainful employment by use of labor-saving devices. These learned professionals may, of course, spend many hours on activity that promotes their learning or prestige, but in even the most exalted callings much time and effort go into housekeeping routines that are amenable to relief by automation.

Impressive amounts of leisure will accrue to the retired worker. If the age of retirement is progressively lowered, as seems likely, and if medical advances keep him ambulatory for ten or fifteen years thereafter, he will have leisure in wholesale batches.

At the other end of the age scale, young people will be kept off the labor market for longer periods of time. Unless medical science develops tranquilizers that one can administer to these young people systematically, e.g., with their orange juice or milk, their leisure may constitute the greatest problem of all.

This is a good time to say something about learned distinctions often drawn among play, work, and drudgery. It is not difficult to become entangled in these notions, because they refer more to a person's attitude toward an activity than to the activity itself. Any activity from which we cannot withdraw when bored is drudgery, and any activity is play when we enjoy it and cease to be solemn about it.

The activities of our waking hours make varied demands upon us. The job makes demands on time and effort—usually stipulated under the terms of the employment. Household membership imposes requirements: the garbage must be emptied, the lawn mowed, and baths taken. Then there are the civic duties of voting, attending meetings, writing letters to the editor, and discussing with our neighbors matters pertaining to the public good.

Finally, there are those moral obligations that we have imposed on ourselves by recognizing them as duties. For example, a young woman believes it her duty to support an ailing and aging mother and to give her companionship. She has created demands upon herself as real and firm as those that might be imposed by a judge.

These activities may be pleasant or unpleasant, or pleasant at certain times and unpleasant at others. What does not change is that they are required. If anything *has* to be done, or if we perceive it as *having to be done,* it is odd to speak of it as a leisure-time activity. Leisure is that situation in which we are free from *all* required activities. Time released from the job may not necessarily be all leisure. The new dispensation will not liberate us from our moral, civic, and domestic obligations. Conceivably we could fill the released time with the routines of fulfilling moral, civic, and domestic duties, but this is a drab prospect. Leisure, it is commonly thought, ought to be enjoyable and interesting. What then can we do to make life enjoyable and interesting in this newly found leisure? How shall we fill the hours that formerly were devoted to earning a living?

The first suggestion that comes to mind is play. The opposite of play is not, as is commonly asserted, work, but rather being serious. Play can and often does require great exertion and close attention. It involves a goal to be reached and is accompanied by excitement as to the outcome of the activity, but once the consequences of winning or losing at games, or of any other activity, become serious, it is no longer possible or proper to be playful about it.

On the whole, people do not play so much as one might sometimes wish. This is understandable, because our lives depend on our being intelligent about means, ends, and consequences. To achieve any sort of security we have to live in the future rather than in the past or the present. To play, as we shall see, is to live largely in the present, and such small segments of the future as we do take account of is for the sake of the present enjoyment. When we are serious, on the contrary, we use the past and present for the sake of shaping a future. The fact of death necessarily makes life serious, because as the Existentialists have so eloquently intoned, it makes the future not only problematic as to its outcome but even as to its duration. Hence death gives urgency and gravity to the present, clothing it with an aura of anxiety and guilt lest we fail to accomplish what we ought while there is yet time. To play or to be playful is to escape this gravity; it is to become carefree, and the occasions on which this mood is becoming to human beings are rare.

The natural time of life for play is, one would think, childhood. But it is only when children are romping about, gaily destroying the lawn, furniture, and the peace of the neighborhood that they are genuinely playful about life. That is why adults rarely approve of children at play. What they do approve of are those imitations of adult activities by children that have no serious consequences. But when children are immersed in this world of make-believe they are probably not playful at all; the odds are in favor of their being serious.

That is why adults and especially educators are forever trying to exploit the so-called play of children. Froebel, Pestalozzi, and Dewey, for example, mistook the natural desire of children to be adults for play. Make-believe adult activities of children can be used to lead them into the real adult activities, but the educative possibilities of a troop of children being truly playful are not impressive.

The adolescent is just irresponsible enough to assume the playful attitude toward life. His elders are scared witless precisely because he does take this attitude toward matters of the profoundest importance, namely, sex, property, and life itself. For the adolescent the opportunities to be playful are numerous, but the restrictions no less so. Hence, adolescent life is not so much carefree enjoyment as an alternation between excitement and boredom. He is thrilled and excited when he is taking chances and bored when he is not. With the help of Providence and the police he manages to grow into young adulthood, when he has to play for keeps. By that time, however, life is a serious affair and no longer a game. Playing for keeps is not truly play.

Of course, the adolescent is still somewhat addicted to the horseplay and ebullience of childhood. Sometimes his pranks symbolize a playful derision of adult seriousness, although it is not always easy to decide how much of this is carefree play and how much of it is a gentle revenge on his elders for their exclusion of him from their domains of seriousness.

For adults the playful mood is a luxury. Employers resent playfulness toward the job; a proper gravity is indispensable to promotion in rank and pay. Employers would prefer the worker to have a sense of dedication toward his work, but they will settle for nothing less than seriousness.

The other duties imposed upon adults—those we have spoken of as moral, civic, and domestic—also preclude playful attitudes; one can never be playful about one's duties.

Where, after all, can the adult get rid of seriousness, utility, and consequences? In his relations with others? But there is scarcely a human relationship that will not be offended to the death by a lack of seriousness. People want to be regarded as persons, as important, in short, they want to be taken seriously.

Lovers may start out by regarding their affairs as a lot of fun to be enjoyed for what it is and no more. This theme has been used effectively in literature, but the social order has never appreciated carefree ecstasy in sex relations. Literature, and indeed the social order as well, would be out of business in a year if such attitudes were generally maintained or tolerated. Friendships can be fun, but they cannot stay that way for long; nor can citizenship, or even membership in a club devoted to fun. In short, when Immanuel Kant enjoined us never to regard persons as means merely, he might have added that they will not let themselves be so regarded. It is difficult to be playful about persons.

Only a few relationships permit us to be playful without incurring serious and even dire consequences.

We can play with ideas. That is, we can entertain them, fashion them, examine them, put them into all sorts of combinations without worrying whether anyone is being hurt or helped by them. Playing with ideas has been a delight to mathematicians, philosophers, artists, and daydreamers of all kinds. Some of these imaginings are never put down on paper or even spoken. Captured by sound or print they can be presented to others for their edification, instruction, or merely for the enjoyment they afford.

The intellectual life is sometimes regarded as a playing with ideas. This is perhaps only partly so, because although the intellectual is known by his inordinate fondness for theory, most of the time he is concerned about how true his theories are, and truth is a serious and not a playful matter. Yet so much of the truth depends on our being able to forget its importance from time to time that intellectual activity comes closer to uniting play and work than almost any other human enterprise. It is because the scientist and philosopher can play with ideas that occasionally something important comes of them. So much is this the case that when we rely on only our needs to stimulate thinking we run the risk of becoming intellectually muscle-bound. That we get results by serious frontal assaults on such problems as atomic fission and disease cannot be gainsaid, but unless some of the earnest young scientists can also play with ideas, the hope for really important advances is slim.

We can play with our sensations. We can savor tastes, sights, sounds, touches, movements, or indeed the "feel" of any experience without concern about how they were caused or what their effects may be in the future. With the usual complement of sense organs we can enjoy or savor any moment of experience. Nature presents her sights and sounds for our delight and artists contrive special objects for our enjoyment. Speaking broadly, all of these objects can be called aesthetic objects and their primary justification or purpose is to enable us to have our sensations without being serious about them.

Yet these objects and these savorings are not wholly without significance. It is true that an automobile or a bus is a means of getting from one place to another, and their significance derives from their ability to get us where we want to go. But are the vehicle and the journey wholly without significance? Do they not have a structure and reality of their own, apart from the goals they serve? Are there not in the skies and fields, in the feeling of good health, in a child's charm, and in the soft texture of a flower delights that need nothing beyond themselves for justification? Is our own experience as we live it not worth a glance on its own account?

Playing with ideas and sensations is an adult sort of play, but children indulge in it, too. It is their world of make-believe, at times so real to them as to cause their elders to be apprehensive. But whereas children combine and recombine their modest store of sensations and ideas and find delight in so doing, only the childish mind can endure them for very long. Adults ask for more variety, for more intensity, for more expressiveness in their mental play. Whether they get it, however, depends on them. Adults who are merely children at an advanced age will also find it difficult to live with their sensations and thoughts for any length of time. Like younger children they will want others to do their playing for them, providing them with ready-made stories, pictures, and songs, easy, pleasant, exciting stories, and enough of them to ward off the ever threatening boredom. Children, young and old, like to be amused, stimulated, excited by others. Becoming adult means, one would suppose, to hoard up within oneself a stock of experience that lends itself to endless variations; that engages interest and quickens the blood; that disengages us from the demands of the practical life and lets us feel the pulse of life itself.

Accumulating these experiences, cataloguing them carefully, discarding the dull and worn-out ideas and images, cherishing the more delightful ones, and learning how to weave them into new life patterns—this, unfortunately, does not just *happen*. This, if we are fortunate and energetic, is the result of education.

Without such preparation what happens to the dearly won leisure? Comes the day of retirement and the elderly couple collect travel folders, make plans, and embark. Strange lands, excitement, novelty, new people, and new languages engulf them. They return healthy and happy, show their movies to envying neighbors and relatives, reassure clucking children, examine their finances, and plan another trip. This process can be repeated, but not too often. There comes the day when planning the next trip itself becomes a duty, and at last a chore.

It finally dawns on all of us—philosophers and plain people alike—that our capacity for being amused and distracted is limited. It takes more and more stimulation to elicit the same amount of thrill and excitement and pleasure. We have to work harder and harder to have a good time.

Leisure, it would seem, is a serious problem. Childish play is no solution because life has robbed us of childish innocence and its childish delights. Adult play with ideas and sensations presupposes long training. Distractions and amusements are fine but they are subject to the law of diminishing returns.

A life of pleasure—high grade or low—created by ourselves or bought at the box office—is not going to fulfill the need of the adult person for satisfying leisure-time activity. Most of us have spent a good part of a lifetime trying to prove to ourselves that we amount to something. We like to feel important because sometimes this means we are important. To be important is to make a difference to something and eventually to someone. This is an ancient bit of wisdom sung by a thousand minstrels, celebrated in countless novels, and solemnly affirmed by philosophy and religion, and by numberless matrons in back-yard colloquies.

This tiresome albeit true observation brings to the fore the problem of leisure, or more accurately, of considerable leisure. How does one remain significant or important when no longer holding a job? For most of us the weekly or monthly paycheck is proof that we amount to something. Without this check certain households would not function. But during our leisure we are not earning the check, and in retirement the pensions come as a result of what we *have* done rather than as a fruit of what we are now doing. Indeed, it has been noted that some retired husbands are worth more dead to their families than alive, thanks to the large insurance policies that they have thoughtfully provided to make themselves dispensable to their dependents.

Yet men and women invariably resent a little the appreciation their usefulness earns for them, although they resent the lack of it even more. The grateful kisses of children, the mother often ruefully realizes, are for services expected. But love that has to be bought is somehow never so satisfying as the freely given article, and it is a happy day for any of us to find even one person who loves us for who we are rather than for what we can do for him or her. There is no greater satisfaction to a parent or an employer or a rich man than to be loved for himself—if only he could be sure.

But whether freely granted or bought, love we must have. Our culture and nature see to it that we shall labor for others to secure that love. If we cannot have the love of those we serve, we settle for their admiration and respect, and if even these are not granted, then we insist that they must at least fear us. This, however, is a sorry state of affairs because it is a far cry from the love we crave.

Our leisure gives us a chance—a second chance—to make ourselves more lovable and therefore to be better loved. For some, as has been remarked, the road is through service to others in fairly obvious ways. Work for the community and organizations devoted to countless good causes, helpfulness to our neighbors, common cheerfulness, good companionship—all these services to our fellows make them love us. They would miss us because they would miss the services we render. They make us feel important because we are important. And because leisure relieves us of the need for being paid in money, we can afford to take our reward in love and gratitude.

One could do worse than to devote one's leisure to serving his fellows in these admirable ways. They require some effort but not more than the average man or woman can muster. They are rewarding because they satisfy our moral urges to serve and they elicit the friendly feelings of those served. Pursued with moderate consistency, they keep us busy and contented.

There is, however, another form of social service which, although less obvious than those enumerated, is at the heart of all of them. It is to present to the world as fine a specimen of humanity as we can contrive. Perfect roses, perfect horses, perfect symphonies, or at least as perfect as man can make these, draw us irresistibly to them. Why? We do not know. Perhaps to say that something is perfect or approaches perfection is to say nothing more than that we love it, want to possess it forever, and yet want to share it with everyone else.

By nature, men are not perfect. Insofar as they approach perfection, they do so with considerable help from their culture. Aristotle, when he prescribed the life of virtue as the preliminary to the happy life, meant no more than to counsel the systematic improvement of man's capacities to think, to make, to feel. By nature all of us have these powers; but only by training and education do we develop any of them to the point where they are first-rate. Some courage all of us have; finely tempered courage only the few have. Some knowledge all of us have; finely tuned intellects only training and care can produce. Any of us can be friends of a sort, all of us can love after a fashion, and we can all appreciate in a way. But to do these things with discrimination and skill takes the connoisseur, the cultivated man.

Romeo and Juliet, Abelard and Héloïse, Tristan and Isolde experienced love as few human beings do. There have also been famous friendships, and how hard the requirements of such rare associations are is nowhere more shrewdly set forth than in Michel de Montaigne's essay on that subject. On a lower plane we have connoisseurs of food, and wine, and horses.* In every instance something far above the average has come into

* About a decade ago Russell Lynes' "Highbrow, Lowbrow, Middlebrow" in *Harpers* and *Life* magazines attracted more attention than one might have expected from a public presumably scornful of connoisseurship.

being because a few individuals cultivated their powers of living well beyond what the average man expects of himself.

Self-cultivation means becoming a distinctive kind of person living in a distinctive way. Although it can take many forms, the cultivated life always presents to the viewer an orderliness, a pattern, a sense of strength under control that commands attention and often admiration. It is life with a style. The life of a Churchill, a Roosevelt, or a Schweitzer has a style that makes it unmistakably unique.

This style of life shines through whatever its possessor is doing: playing golf or dining with friends, working for the community or carrying on research. It is a life with variety enough to make it a source of surprises and a unity that gives it sense and direction. Such a life is a work of art and not an accident.

When a man cultivates his powers to a high order of perfection and binds them together into a total character that reveals these perfections, he creates a human being whom men spontaneously love and admire. To furnish our fellows with such objects of love and admiration is perhaps the most precious of the services that we can render to them.

To such a task some individuals in some cultures have always devoted themselves. They have been few because only a few seem to discern this secret and even fewer can tear themselves away from more spectacular enterprises to pursue self-cultivation. Also it takes leisure—freedom from care about immediate demands of life; freedom from the need to earn the daily bread. Circumstances have not offered this leisure to many and even then it has been paid for by the toil and misery of the multitude.

Perhaps the most famous of the self-cultivators was Socrates, an instructive example for a number of reasons. Although Socrates had freedom from gainful labor to cultivate himself as a moral connoisseur, as a midwife to those who would bring forth new ideas, and as a ruthless examiner of self-deceptions in himself and in others, he was an aristocrat neither by birth, wealth, nor military prowess. On his death bed he had to ask his friends to provide for his children. Nor was he a model of domestic devotion as his wife, Xanthippe, had good reason to know. His wealthy friends and admirers also spent their lives in self-cultivation but did not have to make the sacrifices demanded of Socrates. Of course, the bulk of Athenians had neither the inclination nor the leisure to cultivate themselves.

By now everyone knows that leisure is not the privilege of the few, but what not everyone knows is how some of those few used it to perfect manhood into models that, as Werner Jaeger has noted in his *Paideia,* have never lost their charm for mankind. That this kind of perfection is now open to the many, the many find hard to believe and even harder to strive for.

In another essay we shall talk about the kind of education suitable for self-perfection. Let us close this one by observing that for some people the problem of leisure can never be solved. They are too morally sensitive to use leisure merely for amusement and diversion, but they are not strong enough to undertake self-perfection. For such people there is only one remedy, namely, to take another job. And if no employer can be found to hire them, or if it is economically unwise for them to hold jobs, then let a beneficent government draft these men and women into social service until fatigue and infirmity consign them in good conscience to their rocking chairs.

Education for Leisure

Things are probably not what they seem. Anyone with a taste for profundity can use this as a maxim for satisfying it. If someone says: "Today is a fine day," simply to agree would be superficial. To be profound one must raise questions: "Fine in what sense?" "Fine for whom?" "For the farmer who yearns for rain; for picnickers who do not?"

Socrates by this method convinced posterity, if not his fellow citizens, that what *seemed* to them to be courage, wisdom, and justice were not *really* what they took them to be. Hegel, the nineteenth-century German philosopher, built up a towering system of philosophy out of triads: each triad was made up of three assertions. The first stated what *seemed* to be the case, the second showed that the opposite of the first also *seemed* to be the case. The third statement combined the first two into a statement that presumably was more *really* the case.

This is the dialectical method and it helps us whenever we try to understand anything complicated enough to be important. Complex notions such as life and nature, good and evil, beauty and ugliness, cannot be trapped in any one simple statement. When shrewdly chosen any one assertion highlights some striking feature of what it describes. It ignores other features not so striking. Using a similar strategy, women wisely rely on their more obvious physical charms than on their more obscure excellences of character to initiate matrimonial campaigns.

Wise men, including prospective bridegrooms, on the other hand, become dialectical and operate on the principle that things are probably not what they seem, or at least that what they seem to be is not *all* they are.

On the matter of leisure and the education for leisure, if we wish to be profound, we shall have to use the obvious as a fulcrum to hoist into view facets not usually noted.

In a previous essay this approach quickly disposed of any

simple-minded notions about leisure. We saw that, in one sense, it was not work, but that, in another sense, it was; that leisure was and yet was not play. The upshot of that discussion was that leisure was as much a burden as a boon; that although distractions and amusements seemed to be the ideal way to use free time, they really did not chase the ever threatening boredom away. It turned out that what we needed for our new leisure was a kind of activity that seemed like work but really was not, that seemed like play but really was not. Such an activity we called self-cultivation. By self-cultivation is meant no more than the fulfillment of our capacities to realize values, i.e., to savor life at its most intense and interesting levels.

We are now ready to ask what sort of education self-cultivation requires. Schooling for leisure is a well-aged problem in American education. In almost every set of principles or goals of education committees after years of conferences and deliberation insert "worthy use of leisure."

Intended by this statement, I suppose, was an admonition against the unworthy use of leisure, namely, gambling, heavy drinking, illegally consorting with the opposite sex, idleness, and mischief in general. On the positive side, sports, games, hobbies, and other forms of good clean fun seemed to be called for in the school program.

This seemed like a sensible way of looking at the matter so long as the amount of leisure was relatively small compared to the amount of time spent on the job. With few hours of leisure, recreation, hobbies, and harmless amusements were needed for relaxation. When, however, the workweek is reduced to thirty hours, where in the world is one to find enough amusements and hobbies to fill the leisure hours? Karl Marx made much of the principle that if quantity is increased beyond a certain point, one gets a change of quality. To science this principle is of dubious value, but as an observation about human behavior it is a restatement of Aristotle's golden mean. Courage, for example, is a state of mind appropriate to the total danger situation, so that if you increase fearlessness beyond a certain point, it will in many situations become foolhardiness instead of courage. Similarly, a little leisure is appropriately regarded as time left over from work. But given enough leisure, work is more aptly regarded as time left over from leisure. An even more serious weakness in the hobby-recreation prescription for leisure is, therefore, that it does not take into account the prospect that under the new dispensation life will have to become leisure-centered instead of work-centered. Imagine telling an indigenous Vermonter that the primary meaning of life is to be found in leisure and not in work!

If this reorientation does occur, the schools will likewise have to turn their emphasis upside down. This would really entail a revolution because there is little in the public school curriculum that has not tried to justify its tenancy by its usefulness in the economic, civic, and moral enterprise.

There remain, to be sure, vestiges of the classical languages and literature, of ancient history (which is a never-ending source of fun to some modern educators), and of the fine arts, which have never shaken off the tag of being a frill. These subjects have about given up the fight to justify themselves economically. One doughty schoolmaster insisted during World War II that Latin was a "must" for all officer training, on the ground that Caesar's *Commentaries* would furnish prospective soldiers with all the necessary principles of military strategy. This elicited many chuckles, but no malicious derision—perhaps because some of the military greats themselves had studied the *Commentaries* and had a nostalgic feeling for them. By and large, however, these anachronistic remnants of a classical education hang on by a thin thread of tradition and a kind of shamefaced respect for the venerable men who still teach them. The up-and-coming schoolman has no time for such nonsense.

Even such outcomes as good citizenship play a minor second fiddle to getting ready to earn lots of money in a high prestige position. Good citizenship is urged as important primarily for those whose talents seem too meager to aspire to high prestige occupations. We are inclined to argue that if the boy cannot make money, he ought at least to be virtuous.

Training for distraction and amusement runs counter to our sense of moral propriety. Finishing schools for the children of the rich and highborn may do this sort of thing with impunity, because their mission is to get a clientele ready for a life in which amusement and distraction are serious affairs. Common schools for common men, however, cannot be justified in this way because for common men work and not play has been the primary function of life.

The plain man does not need to study in order to amuse himself; he can patronize the mass media or attend sports events. Hobbies he can learn on his own; most of the fun comes in the learning of them anyhow. He could do with some tuition in certain of the social skills, but whether four years of secondary schooling are required for this is debatable.

Undoubtedly we need schools in order to make people better workers or better men, not to turn out more accomplished loafers and playboys. But to the question of whether the school's role is to train men for jobs or for self-cultivation, history does not give a clear-cut answer.

Schools have always been vocational, if vocational is taken to include everything needed to maintain a certain position in life, for example, that of a gentleman or public official in ancient Egypt, Athens, and Rome. But until earning a living came to require specialized skill and knowledge, schools did not have to distinguish sharply between education for work and for self-cultivation. Once the separation did occur, it was inevitable that schools would put job training ahead of self-cultivation for those who needed special preparation to make their way economically. Today practically everyone is included in this class.

But as so frequently happens, a trend develops its own opposition. Specialized jobs require specialized schooling; but specialization makes mass production possible, and mass production has produced among other countless blessings the new leisure, which, in turn, calls for self-cultivation and a different kind of schooling. So the wheel has taken a full turn, and it is an anti-climax to realize that the education for the new leisure is perhaps not so new after all. It is what has traditionally been called a liberal and more recently a general education, but which more precisely could be called the general studies learned in a liberal spirit. (Cf. the essay on "Liberal Arts and Liberal Education.")

If we are not ready for the new leisure, it is because for several generations Americans have not had much general or liberal education. To get ready for it means getting back to it. It means teaching middle-aged people what they should have learned as youngsters, and it means re-orienting the education of youngsters so that they will not be poring over fundamentals when they are in middle age.

The well-cultivated man is recognized by three sets of habits: the habits of acquiring knowledge, the habits of using it, and the habits of enjoying it. Common education consists of forming these habits, and the well-cultivated life consists of uniting them in a personality that operates with efficiency and style.

The habits of acquiring knowledge are sometimes called the arts of learning: learning to speak, read, write, calculate, and study with some degree of precision and clarity.

In the second place, the cultivated man not only is skilled in acquiring knowledge, he is also skilled in using knowledge to attack the problems of his own life and those of his community. It is one thing to be able to read well and another to read magazines that are useful in informing oneself on how to vote. It is one thing to know how to use the library and another to use it in daily life. The habits of thinking with precision have to be formed deliberately, and school is the place, of course, to form them. One way of judging a school is to examine the amount of such thinking that the pupil is required to do there.

Finally, the cultivated man is not only adept at acquiring knowledge and using it, but he has also formed the habits connected with the enjoyment of it. For one thing, he enjoys the learning process itself because it is no longer laborious and frustrating. For another, by using knowledge he raises his level of enjoyment: life becomes more intense and more interesting. He becomes a devotee of the best, a connoisseur of life and living.

This notion of common education is not unlike that counseled by Montaigne and Locke who were forever asking that the youth be skillful in judgment rather than learned. For the learned men of our time, and indeed of all times, have been and ought to be specialists who make their living out of their learning. Wherever in history we find a high value attached to human self-cultivation, we also are likely to find an emphasis on the kind of education that will turn out men who learn efficiently, who use learning with judgment, and enjoy doing so.

These habits can be formed in only one way, namely, by practice in a wide variety of situations. But they cannot be practiced apart from some knowledge, and because one cannot think without something to think *about* and *with,* there is merit in practicing the arts of learning on those bodies of knowledge that contain the principles relevant to our transactions with nature, other people, and ourselves.

The habits of acquiring, using, and enjoying knowledge are the forms of a general education, and the basic knowledges of the sciences, history, philosophy, literature are its content. Without the form, our quest for value is haphazard; without the content, the quest is superficial.

Educators are forever seeking a set of subjects or topics or books that will give the maximum of coverage in a minimum of time. So far as I know, no real short cut has ever been discovered. The Great Books notion fostered by Mortimer Adler, Robert M. Hutchins, and St. John's

College, the general studies programs at various universities, survey courses, are all examples of this search for devices. Ingenious as some of them are, none of them can dispense with systematic study that requires effort, time, and concentration.

Plans for adult education are a dime a dozen and opportunities for it are no longer rare. It is the willingness to look an educational fact in the face that is rare. The fact is that without the skills of learning and basic knowledge adult education is laborious or trivial. It is laborious if these skills and knowledge have to be sought in adulthood; it is trivial if they are by-passed.

I am not talking now of evening courses in pottery and Shakespeare that afford cultural entertainment. Nor am I thinking of courses that enable plumbers to learn how to install a new type of heating system or courses that permit bookkeepers to become accountants. Such adult education is vocational training. Of adult educational programs affording entertainment and painless culture, on the one hand, and remunerative vocational training, on the other, we have a comfortable plenitude. Of education for adults who want to perfect themselves as human beings there is no plenitude and, what is worse, this sort of education is neither glamorous nor novel.

Education for leisure is education for the middle-aged.

The young should, of course, be busy getting general education which is the foundation for self-cultivation, but it is fruitless to tell them that they are preparing for the leisure of adulthood. Being young means not to be concerned about remote futures. But just as proper growth of bones and muscles in youth prepares them for the tasks of adulthood, so proper general education, whether they know it or not, will function in the lifelong enterprise of self-cultivation.

The aged, on the other hand, are not profitable subjects for leisure education. Old age is not a propitious time for experimentation or for the learning of fundamentals, a few exceptions notwithstanding. Leisure in old age is the time for the harvest of self-cultivation. That is why the uncultivated elder citizens view the future with anxiety. Without the support (psychological, if not financial) of their children and their jobs, they are merely consumers rather than producers of life. In retirement distraction and amusement are about their only recourse.

So long as they have each other, as the saying goes, there are enough common concerns, obligations, and memories to make life endurable. When one partner dies, the other goes through a crisis that more often than not leaves him or her a psychological derelict.

The uncultivated men and women among us are like economically marginal people. Millions of people live each week on the earnings of the previous week. They never accumulate enough capital to weather economic disasters. Two weeks of unemployment, a serious illness, or an accident cripples the family for years, perhaps for a lifetime. Governmental arrangements for social security are no more than a continuation of this marginal existence after regular employment has ceased.

It is not very different with our intellectual capital. Most people get by with a marginal amount—that needed to hold their job and the respect of their fellow workers. The little leisure afforded them could easily be filled by the customary doings and diversions of the group: visiting friends, or foregathering in the tavern, going out to the ball game, playing bridge or watching the movies or television, and taking a trip. One can, of course, continue into old age with the same patterns. Unfortunately, the leisure time is greater and with each year's passing, the companions of one's adult life are fewer.

More and more in old age the so-called inner resources become our only resources. To be with other oldsters helps. Clubs for these senior citizens are being formed, but we have yet to learn how successfully they solve the problems of the aged in their somewhat bitter leisure. To begin with, unless companions can share common memories, association with them is not really satisfying. Even though one can brag about the children and grandchildren in their presence, with strangers there can be conversation, not communion. Communion is reserved for those who had a part in creating the memories that old age musingly revives. That is why perhaps the aged appreciate efforts to transplant them less than well meaning officials and children realize.

Even more important is the fact that the customary way of growing old in our culture has been to preside over the household as patriarch and matriarch. Objects of respect, parents gloried in their children and grandchildren and their ceremonial visits on the holidays and week-ends. The family was as incomplete without the old ones as without the young ones. The respect for the aged was due neither to their power nor to their wisdom and not to their usefulness. It was accorded on the basis of tradition; because they were the accepted symbols of the continuity of the family unit.

The current plight of the aged is due to the fact that they symbolize a discrepancy between productivity and longevity rather than the continuity of a social institution. Unless they can achieve some kind of financial security, they become a financial burden to their children, and unless they can achieve an emotional security, they are a psychological threat to their children. They become the objects of duty rather than of love and respect.

In other words, we face a time when love and respect will come to us even from our kinfolk only if we as persons can command it; they will not come to us unless we are interesting to be with, talk with, live with. They will not respect us unless there is some perfection in us for them to admire. Without a lifetime of self-cultivation, the prospect of becoming such persons in old age is slim. At any rate, old age is too late to make a beginning in this direction.

Middle age, therefore, is by circumstances as well as logic the time for education for leisure. By middle age, our occupational grooves have been cut. Our domestic pattern is fixed. For better or worse, in sickness and in health, there she is or there he is and there they are: children, in-laws, pets, debts, duties, obligations, virtues, and vices.

Furthermore, our talents and limitations are also fairly well etched. That we shall change our mode of work radically is unlikely. Most of us will not become concert pianists, nuclear physicists, or presidents of corporations unless we are already well on the way to playing these or kindred roles.

More important still, our life style has been stabilized around a central motif: the making of money, the making of friends, the discovery of knowledge, serving our community, or exemplifying moral integrity, religious devotion, or aesthetic sensitivity. By middle age we know the areas in which we are connoisseurs and those in which we are duds.

Middle age is a fine time for taking stock. Guidance counselors and a host of ingenious educational researchers have developed inventories and check lists to make this stock taking of the personality a systematic affair. These inventories sample our responses to life and, if they do nothing else, tell us whether we react as do most people or more like the odd minorities called deviates.

More pertinent to self-cultivation is the kind of stock taking that scrutinizes our individual potentials for various types of value experience and what we have or lack in the way of education to exploit these potentials.

For example, Winson Churchill managed to experience values on fairly high levels in many areas. Statesman, man of letters, painter, *bon vivant,* orator, gentleman—there are few corridors of life this man did not explore. No less great a man, Albert Einstein, explored many corridors also, but one would hardly call him a statesman or *bon vivant.* Franklin D. Roosevelt was nearer to Churchill than to Einstein, but his value pattern is in little danger of being confused with either of the other two.

There is a natural wish to be first-rate in everything, because perfection in anything fascinates us. In childhood and youth the ideal of the well-rounded man is the proper one, even if the child demonstrates marked talent and preference in one direction. American parents and youth have been unduly anxious to make early commitments to a vocational future. From the junior high school on, pressure is exerted to have the youngster make a choice because the time of choosing a course in high school will soon be upon him, and because one cannot afford the risk of choosing a course that might later have to be changed.

Let us imagine, however, that we have reached middle age. It is time therefore to resign ourselves to the improbability of becoming a virtuoso on many instruments of life. To become conversant with every area of value and to *know,* at least, what a high level achievement in them would be, are, of course, the minimum essentials of the well-cultivated man; becoming a high-brow in many of them is a different matter. Commitment to such a goal in middle life means a scattering of energies—pulling a weed here, watering a plant there, spraying a bit in another part of the garden—much work and unimpressive results.

A person taking stock in middle age is like an artist or composer looking at an unfinished work; but whereas the composer and the painter can erase some of their past efforts, we cannot. We are stuck with what we have lived through. The trick is to finish it with a sense of design and a flourish rather than to patch up the holes or merely to add new patches to it.

Life is unsatisfying if it is dull, disorganized, or trivial. When life is overpoweringly painful and frustrating it is not only unsatisfying—it is positively bad. However, we are concerned here with something in between the heights of exaltation and the depths of unmeaning misery.

If an artist is asked why a piece of work is dull, he may say that it lacks variety or that it is a stereotype repeated too many times to be surprising. A popular song after ten weeks as a hit is dull on both counts. Its simplicity helped to make it popular in the first place and, by the same token, to make it nauseating after ten weeks.

People whose value potentials are limited to few areas of value, whose speech is confined to a small set of ideas and words, and whose reactions to life are thoroughly predictable, are not interesting phenomena to others or to themselves. When husband and wife realize that there is no point in talking to each other, one can call it either the perfect understanding that needs no further utterance or the complete boredom issuing from the mutual realization that there will be no more surprises in the relationship.

Some pictures and lives are dissatisfying not because they lack variety and richness and surprise, but precisely because they contain so much variety that we can make neither head nor tail of them. People who spend lives of unorganized variety, flitting from one interest to another; who are on twenty-seven committees for twenty-seven good causes; who work on four hobbies at one time; and who are busy from morning until midnight, exemplify the dissatisfaction of the disorganized life. Such a life involves a great deal of activity but does not seem to make much sense. To the actors their lives are tiring; to the beholder they are tiresome.

Such lives need reorganization. They need a commitment to some central motif of value in terms of which all the other activities are selected and organized. It is not necessary for all instruments to play at full volume all the time to prove that the orchestra is earning its salary.

Finally, a life is dissatisfying if it is trivial, if it eternally invites us to ask: "So what?" Some lives signify no great purpose, no great drama, no great importance. But what is there for the average man to be important about? What great events should his life express?

Is it realistic to expect the average man in our culture to be involved in great events? Catastrophes may strike him, but what is the significance of having one's wife and children destroyed by a hoodlum's careening automobile or by a bomb designed for destruction on the grand impersonal scale? It does not even qualify as tragedy, for the only sense it makes is statistical. That is why self-perfection is the last refuge for the common man in a mass culture. He must achieve significance through being something interesting rather than by doing something important. Nothing is so unfailingly interesting as the cultivated human personality —a personality that, in a way of speaking, exhibits the characteristics of a work of art. This achievement does not depend on involvement in earth-shaking events nor does it force us into a mealy-mouthed reassurance that doing one's daily tasks in a cheerful spirit is also "important."

The inventory of our value potentials taken and a commitment to the style of our self-cultivation made, it is time to begin our education for leisure.

Let us suppose that a man in middle age decides that for him the design for self-cultivation requires a study of philosophy and a development of appreciation for serious music. If our man has had a decent general education, he can read both philosophy and music. He already knows the names of the important figures in both fields, their major works, and what the authorities regard as significant about them. Suppose, however, that as a prospective professional man he rushed through his schooling without having acquired the learning skills needed for philosophy and music.

He faces a hard choice. To begin at the beginning in middle age is no fun. Is there no short cut? Are there no courses on television, radio, or somewhere else where one can be told about philosophy and music without going through the laborious processes of acquiring the skills and basic knowledge? The answer is simple: a clear negative.

Let us return to our example. Let us suppose that he does have the basic skills and knowledge he needs to become wise in the ways of music and philosophy. If so, he is ready to begin the exploration of these fields extensively and intensively. It is like exploring a new city of which we know the general layout and design but no more than that.

In the past I have had occasion to visit New York City many times. In general, I am familiar with the distinction of Uptown and Downtown, the main island of Manhattan, and the surrounding boroughs and territories that make up the city. I also know where Times Square, Columbia University, Washington Square, and Central Park are to be found. A few areas I know in detail, but for the rest I have to rely on taxicab drivers or the impatient directions of passers-by. If I wished to become more knowledgeable about New York, I would have to undertake further exploration.

In philosophy, for example, it would mean reading Plato, Aristotle, and many other authors in their own writings rather than in the accounts given of them in textbooks. In music, it would mean listening to hundreds of recordings to attain familiarity with a standard repertory of classical music. It is at this stage of the learning that the formal course is most valuable. The selecting of books to read and music to hear can be time-consuming. Without some plan, it can also be wasteful. A course gives us a prepared selection.

The weakness of such courses lies in the failure of the student to do his homework. Sooner or later every adult education course that is more than entertainment or distraction runs into the fact that middle-aged students have domestic and social obligations that cannot be postponed. Study is done when there is time left over, and there never seems to be time left over.

As a result, the lecturer is listened to with attention until the fatigue of the day makes the eyelids heavy. The discussion is spirited and thoughtful so long as the topic calls for knowledge one already possesses. But when the teacher asks about the books that were to have been studied, there is an apologetic silence.

One of the first principles for leisure education ought to be that it be carried on in leisure time—study, classes, readings, museum visits—and not in time that has to be snatched from domestic and civic duties. If our man has twenty hours of leisure a week, then during those twenty hours let him become a student, or if he chooses to devote only ten hours a week, then let these ten hours be uninterrupted by other demands.

As time passes, the extensive exploration turns into intensive discrimination and study. Having learned the landmarks of the strange city, we can now explore the individual buildings and streets, note their similarities and differences, and begin to form standards of preference among them. This is the beginning of connoisseurship, the last phase of self-cultivation and the beginning of a process that can continue and become more and more satisfying for the remainder of a lifetime.

In philosophy one author is no longer confused with others; in music the style of one composer is as readily discernible from that of another as one make of motor car is from another. It is when small differences begin to make a big difference that we know that we are on the road to self-cultivation. The jazz addict in raptures over a small variation in rhythm, the cook creating a new flavor by adding a pinch of this or that, the reader noting his favorite author's little tricks of style—all are connoisseurs or on the road to becoming connoisseurs.

Connoisseurs may have strong personal likes and dislikes, but a connoisseur can distinguish between his tastes and his judgments. He may have a passion for Verdi's operas and an aversion for Wagnerian operas, but that is not why he judges that Verdi's music is good and Wagner's is bad. The connoisseur devoutly hopes that his tastes will be the result of his knowledge and experience, but he is aware that his judgments *must* be.

Who shall be our guides in the quest for self-cultivation? Who but the connoisseurs? And who are these connoisseurs? They are the men in every age who pass trained judgment on their peers and forebears. These judgments are based on knowledge, experience, and on fine discrimination. Connoisseurs are motivated by a love of excellence that makes them *devotees* as well as *students* of some area of life. The saints, the great moral geniuses, the great statesmen, the great thinkers of each age are the bench marks of history; they are our measuring rods of life.

Each epoch has its own connoisseurs with their own standards. They do not always agree and do not always use the same yardsticks in their judgment. That is why self-cultivation so often asks of us that we transport ourselves into other eras and see them through the eyes of bygone connoisseurs. This is especially irksome for impatient people, but there is no alternative: we can perhaps go beyond the experts, but not without first going through them.

This, then, is the outline of the campaign for self-cultivation for those to whom the future holds out the promise of great leisure. It is after all an unspectacular campaign and there is little that is new in it educationally or otherwise. And yet it should have certain qualities peculiarly appropriate to leisure-time education. For one thing, it should not be too strenuous morally, physically, or intellectually. It should be maintained by interest and the enjoyment that comes from uncoerced success. It should not be a campaign undertaken as a grim duty. Unless the image of self-perfection compels our devotion by love, self-cultivation will have failed as the goal of life. It must charm us into and sustain us through the necessary toil and trouble, as the beauty of the beloved makes every obstacle a glorious opportunity. Self-cultivation should be careful yet carefree. For we are working to perfect ourselves and not to bring about great events, win great fortunes, or achieve great fame.

Liberal Arts and Liberal Education

Commenting on the unsettled state of educational theory, Aristotle noted:

> As things are, there is disagreement about the subjects. For mankind are by no means agreed about the things to be taught, whether we look to virtue or the best life. Neither is it clear whether education is more concerned with intellectual or with moral virtue. The existing practice is perplexing; no one knows on what principle we should proceed—should the useful in life, or should virtue, or should the higher knowledge, be the aim of our training; all three opinions have been entertained. Again, about the means there is no agreement; for different persons, starting with different ideas about the nature of virtue, naturally disagree about the practice of it. (*Politics,* Book *viii*)*

Thus far we are on familiar ground. This is precisely what we are told in virtually all thoughtful observations about education. Everything is in doubt and confusion. But a few sentences later Aristotle makes some remarks that to our minds are far from familiar. After saying that children should be taught those useful things which are really necessary, he adds, "but not all useful things; for occupations are divided into liberal and illiberal; and to young children should be imparted only such kinds of knowledge as will be useful to them without vulgarizing them."

This piques our curiosity. Had Aristotle said that some occupations are better paid or more prestige-bearing or more exhausting than others, we would have understood him, but what could he mean by saying that some were liberal and some not?

Aristotle tells us that "any occupation, art, or science which makes the body or soul or mind of the freeman less fit for the practice or exercise of virtue is vulgar; wherefore we call those arts

* This and the subsequent quotations are taken with permission from the Benjamin Jowett translation in Vol. X of *The Works of Aristotle* published by Oxford at the Clarendon Press.

vulgar which tend to deform the body, and likewise all paid employment, for they absorb and degrade the mind." Now even in Aristotle's day, with slaves available to reduce the freeman's work load, the task of earning a living could not wholly be avoided. And it is perhaps a mistake to overemphasize his remarks about all gainful employment being degrading. It is not the money received that degrades an activity but rather the distraction of the mind from its proper function, which is to cultivate the powers of its possessor. Aristotle does not deny the need for gainful employment; he merely deplores its distortion of what to him is eminently human.

Thus Aristotle points out that even a liberal study becomes illiberal when we apply ourselves to it too assiduously, and that a subject studied for one's own sake or the sake of one's friends or with a view to excellence is not illiberal, but if studied for the sake of others the very same action will be thought menial and servile. It would seem that "liberal" for Aristotle meant *self-determination* as opposed to *being determined* by others or by goals other than the perfection of the self. Liberal education is free in that it is not constrained by a motive other than education itself or self-cultivation.

How do these observations bear on what we call liberal education?

Aristotle's liberal education has generally been interpreted to mean the kind of education suitable only for rich people who do not have to earn a living. With some important qualifications, this interpretation is justified. Certainly people whose time is consumed in earning a living have little time for cultivating their virtues, i.e., their peculiarly human powers of thinking, feeling, and acting. But how rich one has to be to achieve this freedom from preoccupation with gainful employment is another and different matter.

The other qualification according to Aristotle is that we ought not to spend our leisure in amusements, for it would be inconceivable that amusement is the goal of life. Leisure spent in intellectual activity is what he had in mind as the most pleasant of all modes of human existence. However, being rich and powerful, while it provides large amounts of leisure, does not guarantee that it will be spent in intellectual activity or in other forms of cultivating human virtue, i.e., in liberal education.

Taken in this strict sense, it is doubtful whether there has ever been much liberal education. The world has never been able to afford it. Only infrequently does life stop collecting its fees to distribute its dividends. Most of life is spent in trying to get something or to become something; the time for being something—what Aristotle called leisure—is brief and intermittent. Even in Aristotle's day young men of aristocratic birth rushed to the Sophists and paid stiff tuition fees for the kind of training that would make them successful in public life. University studies in the Middle Ages were undertaken primarily for the professional advantages they offered and secondarily for self-cultivation.

Perhaps the study of the Classics in the Humanistic schools of the Renaissance came nearest to filling the Aristotelian requirements. Likewise the studies and spirit of the great English public schools might qualify them for inclusion, despite their role in training young gentlemen for the Civil Service. One may doubt that either the young gentlemen or their masters were *primarily* motivated by vocational ambitions, although there is little doubt that their parents were.

If the subjects called "liberal" have survived the numerous changes in curriculum, it is not because they were studied for their cultural value alone. Greek and Latin did not survive despite the cultural values claimed in their behalf. The humanities have been preserved by being required for a college degree which, in turn, has become a pre-vocational degree. The sciences broke into the curriculum because of their promise of material utility rather than on their intellectual merits. As for mathematics—Plato's supreme mind builder—its lack of popularity is matched only by the respect in which it is held.

There have been times when the "liberal" subjects have been studied as a mark of status not unlike that afforded by travel, and there have been times when the knowledge and eloquence accruing from literary studies were indirectly useful in maintaining one's position in society. Or to put the matter in another way, liberal study requires a certain motivation—a desire to study for the sake of self-cultivation, and not many men in any age are so motivated.

One recalls the typical reaction, not so long ago, of a family in modest circumstances to the announcement of their son that he wanted to attend a liberal arts college for an A.B. degree. If father were a violent man, he would forbid the project forthwith; if of a moderate temperament, the objections would emerge more hesitantly. Both violent prohibition and hesitant objection, however, came to the same thing: how could a young man earn a living with an assortment of grades in English literature, history, philosophy, mathematics, a little science, and some languages?

Would the young man perhaps become a high school teacher? That would make a little sense. Would he go on to medical school or law school or to graduate school? That would make real sense, but could poor boys afford four years of pre-graduate study? Would it not be more sensible to get the liberal education *after* he had opened his office, or secured his teaching post, or brought up his family and taken care of his parents in their old age?

The immediate relatives and friends of the family were, if anything, more blunt and vehement. What *right* did the boy have to demand such sacrifices from his parents? And for what? A profession, an excellent position, a chance to marry into a fine family? If not these, then the boy had no more right to want such an education than he had to want a Cadillac automobile or hand-painted neckties. And if the parents, by chance, condoned the enterprise, the wrath of the relatives turned upon them also.

The boy (or girl) who defied such pressures had more courage than most of his contemporaries and as often as not ended up by fulfilling the dire prophecies of his parents and their friends, for the occupational opportunities to the non-specialist have always been relatively few. Only those fortunate young people whose families could assure them a career in the family firm could afford to plunge into adulthood with nothing more definitive than a liberal arts degree. Today the managers of even the family firm frown upon the scion who did not bother to pick up some specialized training in merchandizing, accounting, or, at least, in public relations.

There was a time, however, when in the liberal arts colleges of our land a young man or young woman who was determined to get a liberal education had a fighting chance of getting it. An aura of leisure hovered about the corridors and old classrooms of these colleges that contrasted with the youthful boisterousness outside their walls. The faculty were living images of those who had renounced gold for a less palpable goal; the more well-to-do professors had their money from non-academic sources but as a rule did not live much differently from their less fortunate fellows.

Even in the science laboratories the apparatus was a little clumsy, smelly, and not very impressive. It would do to demonstrate the principles of physics, chemistry, and biology—perhaps not so precisely as the laboratory manual predicted, but precisely enough for undergraduate purposes.

The faculty was made up largely of men and women obviously devoted to their subjects; some had Ph.D.'s or hoped to get them. When teaching permitted it, an article or a monograph and perhaps a book that would set matters straight in this or that cluttered corner of one's field would grow paragraph by paragraph. One day, given health in the family, a peaceful summer, and a little luck, it would come out, and colleagues would offer congratulations and the Board of Trustees might, who knows, come through with a promotion.

Such low-speed activity, such modest aspirations blending with the low-keyed colors of the academic quadrangle created an atmosphere friendly to the spirit of liberal education. Youth, as Aristotle remarked in his *Rhetoric,* trust others readily because they have not been cheated, and they would rather do noble things than useful ones, and "they are fond of fun and therefore witty, wit being well-bred insolence." All of these characteristics make them susceptible to the charms of human excellence without, however, being charmed by their professors, an attitude that borders on well-bred insolence.

Did these youths acquire a liberal education? How does one know, and how can one tell? Did they cultivate virtue? Were they happy people? And if they did and were, how much of it could be attributed to what they studied during their college years? A manner of speaking, an interest here, a deed there, these alone betray a bygone love affair with this book or that philosopher. Liberal education is a mood and a disposition rather than a result; it is well-being rather than well-doing, and how does one measure a mood?

It is a common temptation to believe that the teachers and courses one recalls most vividly had the most influence on one's life. What if the most important influences are precisely the vague peripheral ones that we never really articulated well enough to remember? In that case, atmospheres, a way of speaking and dressing, might be more conducive to a love of liberal study than a brilliant lecture or a massive library.

It is quite legitimate in vocational education and specialized training to demand forthrightly that the teacher be clear and explicit and that the student be no less so, but there is a kind of self-defeating simplicity about speaking in this way of liberal education, just as it would be odd to ask of a corn stalk in proud array to give an account of itself in terms of the fertilizer, water, and minerals that went into producing it. For growth does not merely summate its ingredients; it transforms them beyond recognition. Liberal education is a growth in humanness, and such growth does not display itself in the recall of so many items in this subject and so many in that.

The only outcome we can expect from a good liberal education is a liberal person, a free person in the modest sense of not being a slave to his passions, to his specialty, to his vocation, to this or that enterprise. In short, he has perspective; perhaps no simpler description of the liberal man is available than that of Aristotle's sketch on the character of Men in their Prime in the Three Ages of Man:*

> They have neither that excess of confidence which amounts to rashness, nor too much timidity, but the right amount of each. They neither trust everybody nor distrust everybody, but judge people correctly. Their lives will be guided not by the sole consideration either of what is noble or what is useful, but by both; neither by parsimony nor prodigality, but by what is fit and proper. So, too, in regard to anger and desire; they will be brave as well as temperate, and temperate as well as brave; these virtues are divided between the young and old; the young are brave but intemperate, the old temperate but cowardly. . . . The body is in its prime from thirty to five-and-thirty; the mind about forty-nine.

And so we must wait, if Aristotle was right, until about the fifteenth reunion of the college class before we can decide whether liberal education has had any liberating effect on our man. This kind of follow-up, guidance officers at colleges are not likely to make. It is not to be confused with the number of the class members who have been listed in *Who's Who,* their average annual incomes, the number of children borne and raised, golf scores, and other statistical information vital to market research.

Yet there was a time, one must reiterate, when the American liberal arts college, especially the fairly well endowed small ones, did seem to beckon youth to liberal education. What is the situation in the latter decades of the twentieth century?

The liberal arts college, to begin with, is still with us as anyone can

* *Rhetoric,* 1390a30-1390b11, trans. Rhys Roberts, in Vol. XI of *The Works of Aristotle,* ed. W. D. Ross (Oxford: The Clarendon Press). Quoted with permission of the publisher.

see. The College of Liberal Arts is still the hard core of even our great universities. The subjects taught in them are still the same: humanities, sciences, mathematics, and languages, plus, of course, many new course titles that fall under these rubrics.

We do not hear quite so much, however, about liberal education. The term "general education" is more common, partly because it connotes what every educated person ought to study for one reason or another and which might more usefully be called "common" education. The reasons given, especially a decade or so ago when the elective system took a bad beating from the advocates of general education, are interesting. One argument was that our educated men and women could no longer talk to each other. So specialized were their vocabularies that outside of the weather, a little politics, and perhaps juvenile delinquency, there was nothing about which they could converse. Because they no longer read the same books, they presumably no longer believed the same verities, and this, in turn, was bound to lead to fragmentation of the intelligentsia.

Another argument had its lever in the fear that the tradition of our Western civilization would sink into oblivion if people ceased to study the humanities and did not at least sample the contents of the great intellectual disciplines.

Still another argument held that specialized education helped one to earn a living, but that the general studies made it possible to live well. Also in this vein, it was urged that the chances for world peace and race survival depended on men of enlightened good will and that specialized courses in electronics or marketing were not fertile sources of either social or individual good will or bad will either.

It is doubtful if all the furor over general education would have amounted to much had not the professional schools come to its aid and made certain doses of it prerequisite to entrance into professional curricula. When a captain of industry in all seriousness announces that the humanities helped him to succeed in the steel business, future executives listen, and if deans of engineering and medical schools announce that English rhetoric, or Sanskrit rhetoric for that matter, is to be a prerequisite for engineering or medical school, the argument for all practical purposes is over.

General education has prospered, therefore, by becoming a gateway to vocational or specialized education. But there is an even more fundamental source of its prosperity. By the strange workings of universal interdependence it turns out that the natural sciences, alone or with mathematics, cannot of themselves run a complicated world. Sanskrit, archaeology, cultural anthropology, and even philosophy, it seems, are needed to cope with problems in communications, public relations, political prognostication, international maneuverings, and foreign aid. Indeed, it would be difficult nowadays to find any course in general education that some ingenious soul cannot show to be indispensable for some great specialized undertaking.

Then, of course, each component of general education is also a "Field" for further study, for specialization up to and through the Ph.D. degree. With vocational possibilities and multi-valenced relevance for all sorts of socially exciting enterprises, the liberal arts colleges are in for good times.

This, it goes without saying, is all to the good. It is satisfying to behold a literature professor living as well as the neighborhood plumber. Given an exploding college population, his tribe may become relatively scarce enough to hoist his salary to compare with those of minor executives in industrial enterprises.

Nevertheless, the problem of getting a liberal education becomes more rather than less perplexing as the academic enterprise prospers. The young man whose plight was recounted several pages back cannot possibly be the center of a dramatic conflict today. What parents would oppose his getting a general education? After all, people are not stupid. The boy could not amount to anything without it. The problem is not to secure parental permission to study for an A.B. degree, but to find a school that will permit one to matriculate.

On the one hand, there is no serious social opposition to the study of liberal arts *subjects,* because they have been certified as somehow useful for vocational success, or, better, for getting the sort of specialized schooling prerequisite to vocational success. Parents and relatives are, consequently, not horrified by the prospect of their children spending time and money on history and philosophy. They may not see the connection between these subjects and success in engineering or accounting, but if the deans of the engineering and accounting schools say there is a connection, who are they to object?

On the other hand, the liberal subjects having lost their amateur standing, so to speak, find themselves with more customers than they can accommodate. The liberal arts colleges are overcrowded and will become more so. Should a young man really want a liberal education, he will have to compete for admission with thousands who merely wish to study the liberal subjects prerequisite to professional training.

Let us suppose the young man is fortunate and bright. He does get into a college of liberal arts—a good one by all accepted standards. That is to say the school has a reputation for attracting famous professors, for sending out graduates who become eminently successful in all walks of life, for having high scholastic standards and a firm moral tone.

First of all, if the young man on a questionnaire or in an interview stated that his primary purpose in coming to college was to cultivate virtue, he would immediately be referred to the counseling bureau. Deviant responses require attention. On the whole, college officials would prefer that he adopt a vocational goal to justify his coming to college. It need not be a firm commitment; on the contrary, in the early stages of the game, a modest tentativeness is becoming to the undergraduate and edifying to the guidance counselor. But nothing in the rules makes it wrong for a young man *secretly* to cherish his quest for studies that *for him* are liberal as well as useful and some that are just liberal. By holding fast to the liberal attitude, he can make a wide variety of studies the vehicles for a liberal education.

In the second place, teachers of the liberal arts courses might also be embarrassed by a student who made his confession to them. This is not because the professor is averse to liberal education for himself or his students. Far from it. There was a time, and he can remember it clearly, when he too had this strange stirring, but this was long ago. Then came graduate study, under a good man mind you, and a promising dissertation on that eleventh-century man. Next, an instructorship with a promise of promotion if he but filled the promise of his dissertation. Well, he did. It was hard going for seven or eight years, but two or three good articles a year, some well-chosen remarks at the annual meetings of his guild, and there he was—a professor. Now he was under contract to write a textbook. He was negotiating with a Foundation for several hundred thousand dollars to do research in a major development of great importance to the Field. With committee meetings, trips to Washington and Burma, workshops in New York, graduate students panting for conferences, there was really little time to indulge in sophomoric yearnings after virtue; self-cultivation would have to wait—at least until after retirement. Well, perhaps a few years after that, because with the shortage of faculty, who knows how long one could visit around on various hospitable campuses.

Now if the student had any real interest in the Field, if perchance he was thinking of majoring in it, it might be wise to look into the matter. Good graduate students were scarce and a little encouragement might launch the lad on a career that might send him also to Washington, New York, and Burma.

If the young man should find this attitude on the part of the professor more vocational than liberal, he would be quite right, but he would be wrong if he jumped to the conclusion that the professor is a foe of liberal education. No, he simply does not have time for it, any more than has the professor of medicine, law, or entomology. He is a specialist, carefully trained in his specialty, which is to train other specialists by day and push the frontiers of the Field an inch forward by night. Keeping in mind that the finest fruits of the human intellect have flowered in the light of this midnight oil and that our proud civilization would last scarcely a year if all its universities were to close shop, no man in his right mind can denigrate the value of research and precise scholarship. Let none begrudge the professors their newly found joys of traveling on generous non-academic expense accounts. It is high time something of this sort happened in Western civilization.

Nevertheless, these developments do not make it any easier for the young man in the hunt for a liberal education. It is like going into a shop over which there hangs a fine sign for "Home Made Doughnuts" and finding that excellent fish and chips were being sold instead. One cannot blame the young man for going to a place that calls itself a college of liberal arts for the liberal education he is seeking. On the other hand, this takes nothing away from the fine vocational education that is now available there. However, it might be less confusing if the signs were changed.

Yet even in these mislabeled institutions liberal study sometimes occurs. Now and then a college is caught with a Ph.D. who collaborates with an occasional student to generate the spirit of self-cultivation. He neglects his research and writing; his telephone never carries important long distance calls inviting him to discussions of important developments in the Field. Through the years he creates a quiet backwater only slightly stirred by the powerful currents of current events. Into it, often by accident, occasionally paddles a student for an interlude of floating—exploring and examining—between episodes of strenuous swimming.

The liberal spirit is also kept alive by the involuntary lapses of those able scholars who have been forced to divert their energies to the cultivation of industry, modernizing backward countries, and keeping their fellow men safe, healthy, comfortable, and sane. They lapse into the liberal mood when their appointment schedules, trans-continental flights, and team research activities create such violent cross currents of involvement that they are forced to spin on their own axis and to reflect upon themselves—for at least fifteen minutes at a time.

Happy is the undergraduate who can catch them at these moments. Without benefit of an appointment; without a terse outline of an "exciting" project, the student can talk and be talked to without guilt feelings that time is awasting. And both are filled with the feeling that this is what both of them had at one time sentimentally thought the academic life would be like.

And so matters have come to a full circle in liberal education. The sort of men Aristotle had in mind as the beneficiaries of a learning that would delight the mind and cultivate their virtues are precisely the men who have no time for such cultivation. And where once the purveyors of liberal education had too few students, now there are not enough professors for even these few.

Is liberal education dead? Yes, if the spirit that animates it is gone. No, if self-cultivation has values that life in our times still craves. What liberal education requires is a class of human beings who want to be free from the pulls and pushes of goals that do not command their full commitment and energy. Complete freedom is, of course, out of the question, but a reduction of pressure might be possible. Who in our time or in the foreseeable future are in position to become the new votaries of liberal education?

The men and women who will seek liberal education in the years to come are not the mighty ones, the important ones, the extremely busy ones. We shall find them, I expect, among the middle-aged and middle-achievement group. These men and women have cut their groove vocationally, domestically, and civically. The man knows that he will not be president of the board, perhaps not even a member of the board of directors. No one will demand that he run for governor, win a Nobel prize, or write the Great American Novel. His aspirations and achievements have subsided into an easy balance. Such men are competent, intelligent, industrious, but they are not destined for greatness in either good or evil. The women in this class have no more children to rear and no more romantic campaigns to wage.

Two fortunate circumstances render the prospect of a liberal education for these people favorable. One is the wealth of opportunities for adult education. University extension programs, municipal adult educational offerings, cultural activities in libraries and museums and half a hundred others are there for the taking without the formalities and red tape of ordinary schooling. The agencies providing adult education are in a better position than colleges and universities to adapt their offerings to the needs and circumstances of the adult learner and are more willing to do so.

The other fortunate circumstance is that the people in the group described as the inheritors of liberal education were forced for a variety of reasons to acquire the rudiments of the learning arts in their high school and college days. Enough history, science, literature, mathematics, and philosophy and the fine arts has probably been retained to make the resumption of study reasonably inviting and feasible. If they had to begin at the very beginning, the prospect would be virtually hopeless, as many an intellectually eager adult has discovered.

It turns out, or it may well turn out, that Aristotle's remarks on education may not be irrelevant to our time after all. The very developments in our civilization—extraordinary technological specialization—that threatened to choke the liberal spirit which Aristotle had made a necessary condition for liberal education has, oddly enough, kept the liberal studies alive, albeit for non-liberal reasons. And the very conditions that made the aristocratic man of leisure anachronistic and otiose have created or are about to create a class of Americans admirably fitted to recreate the liberal spirit. One of the brightest omens of our civilization for the future is that by the most unexpected routes and detours it has succeeded in producing the two factors indispensable to a flourishing culture. One is a group of highly specialized talents to conceive new possibilities for human excellence. The other is a substantial class of intelligent citizens who can actualize these potentialities in their own lives.

Tales In & Out of School

The tales to be recounted in this section are for the most part fictionalized versions of incidents so common that the reader may be tempted to guess at the identity of the characters, places, and events. The names of all persons, places, and events are, however, fictitious and any resemblance to real persons, places, and events is, as the saying goes, strictly accidental. The exception is the essay entitled "Laymen and Experts" the locale and events of which are not fictitious.

Anecdote with Pencils

On almost any morning between September and June one might meet Superintendent Strawman on the main street of the small town whose educational affairs he managed. And at other times of the day also he could be seen on foot or in his automobile en route to one schoolhouse or another. It was often remarked that never had the town been blessed with a superintendent who visited the schools so frequently.

The superintendent was a chunky man with features of no distinction and a history as blameless and colorless as his hair and brows. Only in a small town could he have been recognizable as a personality, and even there it would have taken steady exposure over a long period of time to bring it about. But Superintendent Strawman had steadiness and time to spare.

Whoever stopped to talk with him could not fail to notice a box or two in his hand or beside him on the seat in the automobile. He would explain almost automatically that the boxes contained pencils that he was "just taking over" to this or that school where apparently supplies had run short. There might also be a few packages of composition paper, rulers, or other items that make up the equipment needed in a classroom of a public elementary or secondary school.

This running of school errands would have occasioned little interest were it not for the fact that the school department employed a man to operate a truck wherewith these errands could be run. Surely, mused some of the citizens, the superintendent's time was too valuable to be spent in delivering a gross of pencils here and a ream of paper there. Even the school visits—a sort of educational by-product of the errands—in time caused questioning. Much as parents and teachers appreciated the interest of the head of the school system, they wondered how he could take so much time from making the policy and high executive decisions they had been told were so important in the life of a school system.

Inevitably there arose the speculation that possibly the visits had other than educational motivation, but even the most avid rumor peddlers had to admit that the visits by the strictest applications of Mill's canons could not yield one iota of evidence for romantic adventure. For that matter, the teachers he visited could detect little educational motivation either, for when he did come and deliver the pencils or paper, if indeed he delivered them at all, he made only the usual inquiries as to how things were going, communed a while with the janitor, and departed.

Among co-workers in neighboring communities he was well liked, but whenever his name was mentioned a peculiar look of understanding was evident on every face. At the monthly gatherings of the county's school superintendents, at which the home economics class of the host school staged a better-than-average luncheon, Superintendent Strawman ate appreciatively. A frail but perennial joke consisted of asking Mr. Strawman, "Say, Bill, will you have another piece of pie?" He invariably said that he would, and this released a great deal of merriment in which he invariably joined. Presumably the humor of this interchange lay in a certain bit of history which made uninformed newcomers to the group feel out of things.

Within five minutes after the luncheon was over, and even before the speaker had told his first joke, Mr. Strawman was fast asleep. It was a quiet, unobtrusive sleep, not ugly and yet not charming either. Only children are charming when asleep. But it was restful to see him sleep there at the table, and one might have felt a slight stir of pity had the sleeper been exhausted by toil and trouble. But everyone present knew quite well that he toiled but little; as for trouble, what troubles could Strawman possibly have?

But troubles he did have. When he had been elected to the position everything was promising. A thriving town with enough money for a decent school system and some prospect of growth seemed a good place to which to move from the small district school in which he received his start in the school business. He had had a few ideas, too. He had not been stupid in college and although studying for his master's degree in education had not been the most thrilling experience in his life, it had opened up possibilities of a career both useful and inspiring. He thought he knew good teaching when he saw it, and he had an unexpressed confidence that he could bring out the good in his staff members. Had he been pressed for evidence for these convictions he could not have given any, but then there was no evidence to warrant pessimism about himself either.

At this point in a story, the hero asks himself, "What went wrong?" Strawman did not have to ask this of himself; he knew. It was simply that some men lived too long. One of these was his predecessor, Mr. Dewell.

Mr. Dewell was best described as "a fine man." In a small town this is not a vague description. It connotes certain virtues and denotes certain well-known figures. A fine man is not only honest by ordinary standards and one who leads an exemplary family life but is one who does things for others and for the community. Mr. Dewell was such a man. He had been superintendent for thirty years before his retirement. Generations of townsmen had received their high school diplomas from his hands. He had appointed, with the approval of the school committee, of course, many, many teachers. He had nursed the construction of most of the school buildings from town meeting votes through the dedication exercises. Countless youths, many of whom were now the town's leading citizens, had been counseled and befriended by him.

Above all, he convinced the owners of the town's only industry that each year the schools ought to have more money than the year before. By careful management and saving a bit here and there on salaries—when teachers were in good supply—he was able to inch the budget up year after year until at his leaving he could point with pride at the salary scale of his teachers, the equipment in the classrooms, and the generally prosperous air of the system as a whole.

He knew, as did his teachers and the citizens, that what the owners of the company did not approve could not be had, but not many towns had industries offering such steady employment at such wages—without the benefit of unions.

The owners were not ogres. They were kind, not grasping. They were proud of their business, their product, their employees, their town and its municipal building, its active Y.M.C.A., its modern hospital, and, by the by, its schools, also. But, inasmuch as they paid most of the taxes, they did want to be consulted about the town's finances. Actually they did not really need formal consultation because the town auditor kept the town books in the company's office. The school superintendent was also expected to ascertain the wishes of the company or, better still, to know enough about them not to have to ascertain them.

Why then in such a civic paradise should Mr. Strawman have been unhappy? To repeat, simply because Mr. Dewell was such a fine man and had such good health. For it seemed only natural that when he continued to live in town after retirement his vast experience and wisdom should be utilized in behalf of the fine system he had helped to build. And just by doing the natural thing, teachers consulted him about their problems, the school committee consulted him about appointments and proposals, the citizens consulted him about their children's future, and the company felt that he knew what was good for the town so well that they could leave the supervision of the schools in his still vigorous although unofficial hands. Indeed, Mr. Strawman found himself also consulting him about school matters, which, of course, was the natural thing to do.

To make the consultation process less cumbersome, Mr. Dewell began dropping in on the new superintendent at the school department's offices a few times a week. He joked with the janitor, exchanged greetings with the clerks, and beamed on Mr. Strawman as they discussed problems that the new superintendent thought he was handling quite well.

Mr. Dewell, also out of habit, continued to attend the meeting of the school committee, unofficially to be sure but with fair regularity, and because he was right there in the room, it seemed stuffy indeed not to ask him about the background of this project or that appointment. So he was asked and he told the officials what he knew with his customary fairness and thoroughness. If he, as a citizen, added his opinion as to the best course of action, this was incidental to his role as a "resource person."

So the first year of his retirement rolled around to June when the nights are hot and overscented with flowers, when high school commencements are held. It seemed only natural and a fine gesture for Mr. Strawman to invite his predecessor to continue handing out the diplomas. As one sweet senior said, "I wouldn't feel as if I had graduated properly if I did not get my diploma from him." So she graduated properly that evening and so did seniors in the subsequent years, for there seemed to be no good reason for discontinuing the tradition.

The ensuing decade was filled with instances of Mr. Dewell doing the natural things; the townsmen, the school committee, and the teachers and students doing the natural things. Even Mr. Strawman continued to do the natural things. For example, when his predecessor increased his visits to the school office until it became generally known that he was to be found there mornings from 9:30 to noon, what was more natural than for people to come there to consult with him? What was more natural than for Mr. Strawman to leave him and his conferees to their conferrings?

And so Mr. Strawman left the office in the mornings to visit schools, to run errands, to drop off some pencils here, a few reams of paper there, check on some tests in this school and on the plumbing in that one. In fact, he became an expert on plumbing and no contractor dared to be careless about a repair job, knowing that Mr. Strawman would inspect it not once but many times.

As time went on, a kind of sympathy for the superintendent developed —along with a mild, good-natured contempt—which caused the looks of understanding to sweep over the faces of his fellow superintendents at the monthly luncheons. They wondered what he would do when Dewell died or moved away from the scene.

In the fullness of time, as it was only fitting that so much virtue have a full measure of years in which to exercise itself, Mr. Dewell was buried pretty much as he lived—decently, with dignity, but without éclat.

With his death an era in the town's history ended. He was the personification of the virtues of the middle-class American as they flowered, seeded themselves, and faded in the four score years between the Civil War and the Forties. As a matter of cold history the era had perhaps ended after World War I, but in this little town with its solid industry and stable citizenry the era was carried by its momentum further into time than it was in the cities. Let us say that Dewell personified the dignity of the intelligent, morally firm, and socially responsible man. He believed that earthly rewards were not unrelated to character and that men of substance, especially if the substance had been in the family for a long time, were the exemplars of the good life in a good society. He believed that the well-to-do should take care of the less fortunate—less fortunate in having less money and fewer brains.

He believed in the saving power of education, especially public school education, and he believed that teaching was a calling not a job; that like ministers of the gospel, teachers should be prepared to go without material plenty in favor of spiritual wealth. He himself had lived frugally enough, but even from his meager standard of life he had withheld enough to send his boy to a good college, not in style, but not in poverty either.

But our story is not about Mr. Dewell. What happened to Mr. Strawman after the passing of his mentor? For a while nothing happened. In well-established institutions one can predict that tomorrow will be almost like today. This is possible because institutions operate by rules and precedents and not by whims and inspirations. Mr. Strawman continued to leave his office for the ghostly use of his predecessor and delivered his pencils and papers to the various school buildings as he had been doing for so many years.

But of course there was a difference. It gradually dawned on Mr. Strawman that requests, complaints, and proposals were being made to *him* and that he could not refer them automatically to Mr. Dewell, unless he could find a potent medium to communicate with him. He responded to situations, when he could bring himself to realize that he must make decisions, about the way he thought Mr. Dewell would have responded. Yet, oddly enough, friction increased, teachers met in clusters, citizens grumbled over a post-work beer on the way home, and on a few occasions he thought he detected a sharpness in the tone of the school committee members over this or that matter.

At the monthly county superintendent luncheons Strawman was eyed carefully but cautiously. How would this man behave now that he was no longer in the shadow of his famous forerunner? To some, there did seem to be a straightening of the backbone, a brisker tone of voice, a more incisive statement of opinions. Others saw no change. But they still had their joke about the extra piece of pie and Mr. Strawman dutifully fell asleep within five minutes after the business of the day got under way.

And then it happened. The school committee asked for his resignation, and although tenure laws protected him if he had chosen to fight the ouster, he did not so choose. Dazed and puzzled he did resign—not more than eighteen months after the decent and dignified death of the beloved Superintendent Dewell. If Strawman was stunned, he was in a numerous company. Everyone was stunned. Teachers, parents, schoolmen in the county—indeed even the school committee itself could scarcely believe that it had happened.

But what actually had happened? That was the strangest part of all—nothing happened. At least nothing that had not been happening for nearly forty years since the day Mr. Dewell became superintendent. The kindly, well-meaning efforts in behalf of the citizens, the teachers, the pupils, and the school committee to which Dewell had devoted his life were just more than the beneficiaries of the kindness could take.

Teachers were sick of a salary schedule that was not bad, but nowhere as good as the conditions and finances of the town warranted. Parents were tired of sending their sons and daughters to colleges suggested by Mr. Dewell, and the school committee was apparently tired of waiting for Mr. Dewell's considered judgment before hiring personnel and letting contracts.

It must occur to the reader that these rebels were not sick of Mr. Dewell but of themselves, and if they had been asked whether they hated Mr. Dewell, they would have been horrified and quite sincerely would have denied it. But it rarely occurred to anyone to inquire whether they hated themselves, and so matters had to wait upon circumstances before they could be clarified. These circumstances were in a way complicated and yet they did not seem to add up to their explosive effect. One could find other communities in which more potentially explosive causes fizzled out into nondramatic consequences. To be sure, there was a series of events that led up to the climax, but why they were not nipped in the bud or shortly after their burgeoning is a puzzle, unless one keeps in mind a much longer chain of events, namely, the one instituted when Mr. Dewell became superintendent two scores of years earlier.

To begin with the more obvious causes: it happened that because of deep and complex sociological factors the high school faculty had come to include a number of young men, most of whom were already married. Understandably, their school salaries could not provide baby food, pediatricians, housing, and clothing appropriate to the life of a school teacher, modest as these were. So some of the young bloods began to grumble about salaries.

This in itself, while unusual in so well ordered a system, was not without precedent even under Superintendent Dewell. Two factors, however, poisoned the situation. One was the rebellious spirit of the ringleaders. Not only did they want more money, but they injected into the demands a note of indignation and anger that sounded discordant beside the customary appreciation of the staff for the beneficent town treasury which had not depressed their salaries appreciably below other community pay scales.

For some reason the ringleaders assumed that Strawman, like Dewell before him, would be shocked at the thought of teachers taking an aggressive initiative against a benign school committee, a benign superintendent, and a benign citizenry including a benign company that made the whole enterprise economically viable. They could not be blamed for thinking so; yet they were wrong. As a matter of fact, Strawman had hoped they would come to him for leadership in their demands. It would have been the sign of their acceptance of him as an executive. Instead, another factor helped to isolate him from the movement.

This was his habit of visiting the schools with his pencils and other supplies. Because he would drop in on no particular schedule and for no particular reason, he interfered, without knowing it, with intrigues and conspiracies. So he became "Snooper" Strawman, symbol of the powers who were supposed to be enemies of the pay demands. Consequently, he was excluded not only from the "secret" meetings which everyone knew were taking place, but also from the formal meeting of the teachers' association assembled to vote on the matter. Pride prevented his attending uninvited, and this was really too bad, because had he gone and spoken, the affair would in all probability have taken a different and less sensational turn.

The reason for this was to be found in the composition of the teaching force. The time had not yet come when large proportions of the teaching staff were married women or men. Many were maiden ladies whose simple wants were adequately met by their salaries. Many were sisters still living in the parental household. Although nobody in their family commanded a high salary, the combined earnings of three sisters and a father enabled all of them to live in a good house, drive a decent automobile, and even do some traveling in the summer. Perhaps these ladies would have chosen poverty-haunted marriage over their comfortable single state, but as between their comfortable single state and the uncomfortable one of getting into war with the school committee they plumped for the comfort. In any event, there was no enthusiasm for war of any kind, and yet when it came to a vote they were persuaded by the young males to throw their lot in with the warriors. Strawman could have had their support had he been there.

By this time people were taking sides for or against the demand for higher pay. The teachers' petition had not yet been drawn, much less presented, but the local paper editorialized on what it would mean to the tax rate, and a rash citizen sent a letter to the newspaper to the effect that the company, having made more money last year than ever before, could afford to pay more taxes in return for a stable and cheap labor supply. The writer was identified as a recently hired worker and further inquiry disclosed that he was a union organizer sent in to bring sorrow and strife to the contented workers. The spectre of a labor union aroused the local merchants and also, for some unknown reason, the executive officers of a famous patriotic society for ladies.

Within a few weeks, it seemed, the peaceful town was stirred into factional accusation and counteraccusation. The pupils were enthusiastic about the strife, expecting that there would be enough excitement to make the teachers forget the routine of lessons and homework. Teachers, though still presenting a strong front, inwardly worried lest reprisals leave them without jobs; the struggling wives of the ringleaders perhaps worried more than the others.

Amid all the excitement, where was Superintendent Strawman? Superintendent Strawman was right in the middle of everything, but just as in the center of the whirlpool there is a minimum of motion, so was Mr. Strawman strangely uninvolved in the furor swirling around him. How could this be?

Clearly because all the parties involved were acting on what they knew Mr. Dewell had done in similar situations and what Mr. Strawman would do in this one. Mr. Dewell, the company officials and the school committee knew, would have invited the ringleaders to his home on a Sunday evening at the first signs of trouble. There would be coffee and Mrs. Dewell's superb homemade doughnuts and before an open fire some man-to-man talk would sooner or later take place.

Mr. Dewell would hint delicately that perhaps a few subprincipalships might be vacant next year, or that the football or basketball coach could use some part-time help at extra pay. The inference that some of these energetic young men would be logical beneficiaries of these windfalls was unavoidable. If this maneuver did not calm the troubled waters, Mr. Dewell could be counted on to invite another group on another night; a group that contained rivals of the ringleaders, and he might let it be known that this group could assure the teachers that a raise of some kind would be forthcoming. Naturally, the available promotions might also be mentioned. The importance of being reasonable would be discussed at length. Perhaps the money that the town voted would not give the teachers all they were asking for, but there would be some, and had not his promises always been redeemed in the past?

The teachers and the school committee, for their part, knew that Mr. Dewell would have managed to discuss the situation with the officers of the company; perhaps after a meeting of the Library Trustees, or after a church social, or at the bank. He would have sounded out the prominent citizens controlling the votes needed to swing appropriation measures at the town meeting. Without missing a stride or a smile he would have the situation well in hand, and, by and large, to the satisfaction of all concerned.

Was this chicanery? Was this double dealing? Was it politics in any bad sense? Hardly. It was human relations engineering, to be sure; it was paternalism; it was trimming here and compromising there. It was, in short, an unscientific but quite effective way of so structuring a situation that all concerned could see favorable possibilities in it. He asked and got nothing special for himself; he was a partisan only in the sense that he honestly believed that those in power deserved to have that power. Because this was a limited vision, and because a sincere devotion to it guided his moves, Mr. Dewell was as predictable as the tides. But it was this very reliability that proved to be Mr. Strawman's undoing.

For what everyone seemed to forget—and Mr. Strawman made it easy for them to forget it—was that Dewell was dead. In fact, Mr. Strawman was doing none of the things everyone believed he was doing, or rather that he would be doing, if he were Mr. Dewell. He was, after all, still Superintendent Strawman, the man who moved when Mr. Dewell gave the instructions, and without these instructions he did nothing. He did not approach the company officers, he did not call in the ringleaders for a Sunday evening man-to-man talk. He waited to be asked while everyone waited for him to act. In the meantime, he delivered pencils to this and that school.

And so events rolled to a climax. The petition was presented by an irate teacher delegation that made threats it had no intention of carrying out; solid citizens made accusations they did not mean; parents were unhappy about the unwholesome excitement surrounding the schools, and the officials of the company were outraged at the turn affairs had taken.

"In these circumstances," the chairman of the school committee explained to the press, "Superintendent Strawman's usefulness to the school system has been seriously impaired and all interests would be best served by his resignation."

Mirabile Dictu

About miracles modern men are prone to overhasty generalization. Either they regard miracles as the irresponsible intervention into the affairs of men by supernatural powers and therefore to be summarily dismissed as superstition, or they go to the other extreme and marvel at the wonders wrought by scientists and accord them the reverence ordinarily reserved for the Divine.

A more modest attitude would define miracles as events for which no cause can be assigned, at least not at the moment when it is being sought. This attitude, I submit, restores to the miracle a useful status in daily life where events whose causes we cannot ascertain and which have an impact upon our lives that is peculiarly fortunate or unfortunate occur frequently. After an airplane disaster reporters ferret out the names of persons who had scheduled passage on the ill-fated craft but who failed to board the flight for one reason or another. One had forgotten something in the checkroom and returned to retrieve it. Another was not aboard because he had one too many cocktails, and still another decided at the very last moment to return to his wife instead of seeking a new life elsewhere. These escapes are properly regarded as miraculous, because their cause is mysterious or hidden from us, and also in that they intersect our life plans as if they were designed to fit in positively or negatively with them.

The miraculous, in the sense I am proposing to use it, is a blend of ignorance and chance that is far more potent in the conduct of life than knowledge and design.

Civilization and education, it ought to be noted, are consistently on the side of knowledge and purpose and against ignorance and chance. This is as it should be, save for the circumstance that increasing knowledge and purposeful action does not necessarily decrease the volume of life controlled by ignorance and chance. The reason is simple: every deliberately instituted act—driving to the shopping center to buy groceries, for example—sets up chains of events other than and in addition to those that result in buying the groceries. For example, one waves to the postman on the way, or one inadvertently fails to return the greeting of a diffident student. These events in turn set up their own chains of events that in turn intersect with other chains. Theoretically one could calculate all of these adventitious results before undertaking an action, and perhaps with pocket electronic computers we shall one day be aware of all the consequences of our own acts. Shall we also be aware of all the consequences of all the acts of everyone else? Can we look forward to becoming computers orbiting about the Computer of Computers?

The schools, being on the side of knowledge and foresight, are naturally not the best place for human beings to learn to cope with the miraculous. Or to be more precise, the school is not a good place to learn how to adjust one's life to the miraculous, for, strictly speaking, one can do little with the miraculous but adjust to it. And yet the school perhaps misses a good bet in not paying more attention to those adventitious events that have changed the course of history. For these are the really interesting items and not the logically obvious ones. They transform the causal chain into a drama.

In general, schoolmen interpret the miraculous as a Divine intervention into terrestrial affairs and consequently are reluctant to give it room in school affairs. Not being sufficiently respectful of ignorance and chance, they seek causes for everything and infer them long before the data warrant their doing so. So while denying the miraculous, they often strive for goals that it is impossible for them to achieve in their current state of knowledge or control. In other words, they strive for the impossible precisely because they deny the reality of honest-to-goodness, everyday miracles. Among these miracles are the influences of a teacher on a particular pupil at a particular point in his developmental history.

Every man when in a suitable anecdotal mood can relate an incident that inspired him to unusual effort. For one man it was a hero in life or in literature; for another it was a woman; occasionally a parent or a teacher was the trigger that released enormous energy in behalf of some cause or other. Sometimes, however, it was not a person as such who effected the change, but rather an event or a situation.

Quite frequently, one might suppose, these dramatic motivations occur in school. A schoolman, one might also suppose, would almost sell his soul to find the secret springs that give these motivating events and persons their power. This secret would indeed be the pedagogue's philosopher's stone. Its touch would transform a reluctant schoolboy into an inspired learner and, correlatively, transform teaching from drudgery to a kind of inspirational magic.

Psychology, especially educational psychology, disdaining all mystical nonsense, has offered us a number of formulae in terms of which the pedagogue can so program his instruction that the hidden springs of motives will be released—not mysteriously but by design. To this end, lists of motives, instincts, interests, drives, and needs have been prepared. They show, for example, that at such-and-such an age, the boy will naturally love to play war games and the girl with dolls.

These developmental schedules are not without their use. They prevent the beginning teacher from becoming ridiculous in that they indicate the "normal" incitements to adequate school behavior. They help in choosing literature for children, as well as toys and games, appropriate to their needs, interests, etc. They are reliable because they represent interests that children have actually displayed and not the observers' ideas about what the children ought to be interested in. Finally, a child whose tastes in these matters is noticeably deviant can be cut out of the herd, so to speak, for special study. Nevertheless, these interest schedules do not tell us about the more dramatic transformations of a child's life in which the whole aspirational schema is radically changed.

Of less use to the pedagogue are the more general theories of human motivation. For example, it is now customary to invoke the principle of security as a means of diagnosing children's difficulties in school. Unfortunately, feelings of insecurity can be used to explain equally well such diverse behaviors as extraordinary scholastic achievement, scholastic failure, undue devotion to one's parents, and abnormal hostility toward one's home.

Will a teacher who makes a child secure inspire him to a significant change in his motivational pattern? Or will a teacher who destroys a child's security inspire him to unusual achievement? That depends, one is told, on the nature of the child and presumably on the nature of the teacher also. So there seems to be no easy substitute for studying the child, the teacher, and, one might add, all other relevant circumstances in their particulars. But is it the duty or is it within the competence of the teacher to undertake such clinical study?

Those who argue that teaching is an art rather than a science probably have in mind this difficulty of predicting pupil behavior from general principles. The artist is never sure ahead of time just what impression his work will make—even on himself. He is guided more by what the work already done requires than by the prescription of a set of rules. Teachers work on a similar basis. One tries a posture, approach, or gambit and a sense of rapport ensues that seems to call for this question or that remark. Did it come off? Who knows? Many years later one may find out that for a certain student it did, but more often it turns out to have been one of those ineffectual tries that sank into pallid oblivion.

Schoolrooms go on from day to day not by dramatic successes but by routine. These are the standard tasks and expectations that provide momentum to sustain the engine between piston strokes of inspiration and insight. Nor are the lives of pupils a succession of red-letter days. One of the more damaging misconceptions of prospective teachers is that they must have exciting lessons every day. Both the Progressives and the Idealists foster such an illusion, for both are given to enthusiasm and find it hard to pace themselves through the less exciting intervals of life.

It is perhaps a truism that a reliable combination of routine and variation makes life interesting and therefore endurable. But it is less obvious that teaching, when one becomes sufficiently self-conscious about the surprises latent in even its most routine moments, has a more intense fascination, an almost frightening fascination, than most occupations. For in no calling are the results of what one does so pregnant with possibilities for the pupil and yet so unpredictable—unpredictable as to the person they will affect, when the effect will take place, and what it will be.

There come to mind two examples of influence on young pupils that may make some of these abstract remarks more concrete.

The first is that of Katie. This lady was an eighth-grade teacher in a fairly large school. The other eighth grade was under the governance of a Miss Belinda. Both women were past middle age. Katie was known as a tough teacher and her colleague was known as a gentle, lovable teacher who was "as easy as pie."

As the end of the seventh-grade year approached, pupils began to wonder to which of the eighth grades they would be assigned. Nobody knew the principle of selection, and in those days parents would have been backward about trying to influence the authorities in such affairs. In any event, the pupils believed that some impersonal fate allotted them to the lioness or to the lamb.

With the girls the hope was pretty generally in favor of the lamb. Not only would there be a less threatening atmosphere so far as studies were concerned, but romance would not be so rudely suppressed as it would be by Katie's rough tongue. The girls knew, however, that some of them would land in the lair of the lioness, and for them the last day of school was a day of doom. As each girl learned her fate, dejection or elation was spelled out eloquently on her face.

Among the boys the sentiments were less uniform. Some, like the girls, dreaded a hard taskmaster, especially if their scholastic caliber was not high. The more gentle temperaments dreaded the austerity for which Katie's room was noted, but other boys looked forward to Katie's eighth grade as a trial of their manhood, both of mind and soul: of mind, because a good report card from Katie was about as clear a sign of scholastic distinction as the town could provide; of soul, because to take the tongue lashings, the whippings, and the other cruel and unusual punishments for which Katie was notorious was something like surviving basic training with the United States Marines. For young men of this mettle the great fear was that they would *not* land in Katie's room. Certain it was that there were only two kinds of men: those who had gone through Katie's room and those who had not.

One entered her classroom in September with teeth clenched waiting for the blow. The long assignments came as predicted. The sharp rebukes for mistakes were duly delivered; there were some sharp hand rappings. But one waited all year for Katie to throw her famed dictionary at the class tough; one waited in vain for the cruel and unusual punishments.

It is hard to say whether the boys were more relieved or disappointed. It would not do, of course, to reveal the true state of affairs to outsiders. On the other hand, the more daring lads who were tempted into overconfidence by the unexpected mildness of Katie's demeanor were set upon so firmly and so promptly that her reputation remained secure. The truth of the matter was, of course, that the alleged horrible goings-on in Katie's room had been invented by generations of schoolboys as a tribute to their own imagined toughness, and each tale expanded with every repetition. Thus it was that when men who had been Katie's pupils asked each other whether they remembered the time when Katie had whipped every boy in the room, or when one boy had been forced to read out loud for two hours at a stretch, nobody could recall the incidents, but they were ready to believe that they had occurred. Indeed, with the years Katie's opportunities for sadism were radically reduced by the fact that her authority was less and less frequently challenged.

Pupils learned a great deal in that one year and some for the first time discovered how much work they could do and how satisfying scholastic achievement could be. It was an exciting year not because they learned exciting things but because they were living, they thought, dangerously. So great was her reputation that such activities as part singing, drawing, and reading aloud from Webster's orations (with expression) were transformed from sissy stuff to more or less manly exercises.

Many teachers tried to build a similar reputation and most of them failed miserably. Perhaps because they did not have her gray hair, her black neckband, and pince-nez. Perhaps they lacked her inward self-assurance. Above all, they probably lacked her authenticity, for Katie never tried to build a tradition. She was herself and the tradition grew about her as naturally as did the grayness of her hair. For all one knows, many a boy or girl was thoroughly miserable in her classes and was too frightened to learn much of anything; but this possibility (or actuality) somehow never became part of the tradition.

In modern parlance Katie's room exemplified a fairly pure form of what the late Kurt Lewin called an authoritarian school atmosphere. The teacher made all the assignments without consulting the pupils. She issued commands and made demands; disobedience was immediately and not gently punished. There was a minimum of interaction among the pupils; whispering, when she chose to be aware of it, was a major offense; passing notes was a pastime so dangerous that only the toughest pupils ever engaged in it. As for her method of teaching, perfect reproduction of a model response was all she knew. Whether it was arithmetic or part singing, spelling or declamation, everything had to be done just as she wanted it done. She had only a blackboard, some maps, and the textbook as teaching tools. She was, in short, an exemplar of every sin in the pedagogical decalogue.

And yet, in another sense, she was an exemplar of nothing because she created a unique sort of authoritarian atmosphere in which the hardy ambitious pupil could test himself by a criterion that his peers accepted. It was also a haven for the compliant, docile child, who became more so during his year with Katie. It was an exciting authoritarianism, a rigidity with a difference, with almost a hint of the splendor that military rigor sometimes acquires. She was not fussy or nagging; she was neither conspicuously kind nor unkind.

The point of all this is that Katie and her methods could not be reduced to a formula which could then be judged pedagogically good or bad, any more than a particular painting can be judged good or bad simply because it was done in the Romantic style. For some pupils it worked wonders; for others it was disastrous. What schools in her day lacked was the ability to make a good guess as to which pupils needed Katie and which should be steered away from her, and one is far from sure that schools have made any considerable progress in matching pupil-styles and teacher-styles.

The second example is furnished by an incident that occurred in the seventh grade to a young chap who had come to this country when he was seven or eight years of age. By then he had been thoroughly acclimated and had settled down to an uneventful passage from grade to grade. His marks were neither poor nor good. His parents accepted his achievements as about suitable to his talents. It was a nice adjustment all around. Then one day the children were asked to write a theme or composition about some event in their lives that they thought was interesting and significant. Everyone chewed pencils thoughtfully and there accrued the usual bag of themes about a visit to one's aunt in Cleveland, the dog who was nearly run over by a trolley car, the new bicycle, how to make an electric bell, a birthday party. The papers were collected by the teacher and life went on as usual.

Perhaps a week or even two weeks later the principal, a youngish dark man by the name of Halloran, entered the room, held a whispered conversation with the teacher and began to read a composition.

It was a limping tale about a sea voyage on a passenger liner. In those days, near the end of World War I, there were still many immigrant children in school, and it was not at all surprising that some of them would remember the trip across the ocean either as a traumatic or nostalgic episode in their lives. With some sense of drama, Principal Halloran delayed announcing the authorship until the end of the reading. The revelation caught everyone, including the author, by surprise. The author, of course, knew it was his composition but he was no less puzzled than his classmates at the distinction bestowed upon his literary effort. For one thing, his immigrantish oddness had long since worn away and he was thoroughly Americanized in speech, dress, and all the minor vices. For another, his accomplishments in school were so indifferent that this honor seemed thoroughly out of character.

From that day on, however, he regarded himself as a writer and began to take on the behaviors of a student as well. At the Memorial Day exercises he was selected to render the Gettysburg address and thereafter each teacher referred to him as the boy "who could write."

In high school his compositions became concoctions of bombast and undue solemnity, but he was named editor of his school paper, and in college at least one of his English professors encouraged him to write. One of his efforts achieved the distinction of being rejected by the late Henry Mencken with the notation "has some promise." He was salutatorian of his class in high school, valedictorian of his class in college, and voted the man most likely to succeed (at what was not specified).

He did not fulfill the prophecy, at least not in the field of literature. He did not return to class reunions often enough to enable his classmates to make a proper appraisal of his accomplishments. Nevertheless, the episode on the afternoon the principal read his little composition about a sea voyage was as critical a point in his life as the discovery that she is beautiful is to an adolescent girl.

As for Principal Halloran, he left the school system at the end of the year and was never heard from again. Not that he disappeared or took up a life of crime, but for the seventh graders he ceased to exist when he left the school system. One cannot be sure that the results of his gesture were ever made known to him; one hopes they were. Being the person he was, he no doubt repeated this gesture many times in his school career, and one is tempted to capitalize on the episode described here by urging teachers to read the compositions of indifferent pupils aloud or persuading the principal to do so. But who would be willing to predict the results of such readings?

Indeed, the lessons of Principal Halloran and Katie may be quite different from what at first glance they seem to be. It is not that they furnish paradigms of teaching or that they exemplify any profound teaching principles. Rather, they exemplify the frightening fact that in the act of teaching we create situations and stimuli whose consequences are beyond calculation, even if it occurred to us to calculate them.

When such small behaviors produce such great results, who is to blame a teacher for trembling with anxiety at the close of each day? What remark, what gesture, what grimace, what quip, what praise, what reproof produced what effects on which pupils? And what effects will tomorrow and the day after that engender?

The engineer responsible for the structural integrity of a huge span, the surgeon whose every movement is significant, the general with thousands of lives at his command are familiar symbols of vast responsibility. We wonder at times how these men bear up under it. Yet a teacher—not a mighty person on any scale—daily radiates influences on many many children. The engineer has control over what is being built; the surgeon sees the effect of his movements; the general, one hopes, takes only well-calculated risks. The teacher, however, is often playing blind man's buff, not knowing whom he touches and how the touch is received. Responsibility in such a situation takes on a tinge of desperation.

Mercifully not many teachers are like Socrates, who could never forget the gravity of the teaching relation, who so carefully desisted from letting himself intrude into the learning process. He was the midwife merely helping the pupil bring his own conceptions to birth. But it was an impossible role. His pupils could not help learning Socrates as well as themselves. Perhaps it is wrong to say that we teach subjects, and it is difficult to understand what is meant by saying that we teach pupils, but the teacher never fails to teach himself to the pupil.

That is why teaching machines may well take over the bulk of instruction in the years to come. Even the best of human teachers is not an efficient teaching machine. All that a human teacher can add to the mechanics of instruction is himself, his peculiar organization of experience, which, fortunately or not, is induplicable. His thoughts are not merely true or false; they are profound or shallow, significant or trivial, interesting or boring. Most important of all, he is a source of praise and reproof.

It is also fortunate that, by and large, school teachers do not reflect on the peculiar responsibilities they bear and, aside from an occasional shudder, they manage to ignore the effects of themselves on their pupils.

Only in this way can they concentrate on the routine of instruction and school keeping.

Perhaps responsibility, like our clothes, when continually worn loses its weight. Men's work would cease altogether if their gaze were forever inward, brooding on the possible consequences of their acts. Blessed are the routines that make so many actions so automatic that they no longer need thought and reflection. Like other professionals, the professional teacher becomes aware of responsibility only in critical situations.

Certainly it would be an unsubtle teacher who would wear his care upon his sleeve and allow his pupils to sense his anxiety. Sören Kierkegaard, the Danish theologian, never tired of asking about the mien proper for a genuine Christian. If a true Christian were to avoid pride, over-confidence with respect to salvation, false humility, the escape mechanism of monasticism, smugness, meddlesomeness in the name of neighborly love, and a half hundred other demeanors incompatible with the Christian spirit, just how should he behave?

Kierkegaard's answer was long, dialectical, and overly subtle, but roughly stated it came to suggesting a kind of disguise, an outward mien that belied the inward questioning, anxiety, and concern. And perhaps something like this is the unhappy answer for the genuine teacher as well.

It means that teachers cannot hover like mother hens over their little charges, nor does it mean a prying concern for the home life and private concerns of the pupil. It does not mean a sentimental "love of children" or being a pal to teen-age boys. To none of these roles is the teacher uniquely essential. Yet when we ask for something positive, there is no one image to recommend, just as there is no one image appropriate to the genuine Christian spirit.

About all one can say is that the teacher, first of all, must be himself, and, second, that he be concerned about the pupil, but in a peculiar way. He is himself *for* the pupil, while his concern for the pupil is disguised behind a concern for a subject of instruction. Thus it looks as if Teacher X is teaching arithmetic, but his concern, as Rousseau pointed out, is what is happening to the pupil when he has an arithmetical insight. In exemplifying a genuine human perspective of life, the teacher must seem to be wholly unconscious of being an example.

Perhaps this is a roundabout way of stressing the inward dimension of life whenever the transaction is between persons rather than between persons and things, which is sometimes called "subjectivity." It is that reflexive power by which the person's experience is split into a content and an awareness of that content. The content can be classified and described; it is what we have in common with our fellow men; it is what psychology and sociology can study. With the awareness of the content, matters stand otherwise. Because the individual's experience is growing from moment to moment, how he receives each new moment is a unique creative occasion in history. However intelligible it is after the individual has acted and added an item to the content of his experience, at the moment of receiving the future into the present he is in spiritual solitude. Hence many of his acts are miraculous in the sense of the word that has been described.

It is almost impossible for one individual to express his subjectivity directly, his peculiar way of receiving the world. If he tries to say it in ordinary language, his words become universals and they describe not him alone but the experience of mankind in general, for they describe what is common, not what is individual. As we try to communicate our attitude toward the world we are beset by doubts and hesitations. Are we being unduly modest? Or falsely so? Are we seeking sympathy? Are we trying to save our ego at the expense of others? In short, are we telling the truth about ourselves?

At such times a poem, a song, a picture may express better what it is we feel than words, and occasionally, if we are fortunate, we can *act* out what we feel; we exhibit ourselves instead of describing ourselves. Such manifestations have a strange power over the beholder. What I mean here is akin to the effect upon us of the complete authenticity of a child absorbed in some act, or an adult in that rare moment when he has forgotten that he might be observed.

At other times we resort to indirect communication in the form of irony, the parable, the comic, the paradox, the dialectical. In these forms of speech things are suspended between opposites, between the literal and the figurative, the particular and the general, the comic and the tragic, the sublime and the ridiculous. Such a communication communicates nothing in the strict sense of the word, for it is logically a kind of nonsense. Yet it arouses in the hearer the emotional state the communicant wishes him to have.

Perhaps the teacher also communicates indirectly; perhaps this indirectness is what mocks every attempt to formalize a Katie's or a Halloran's influence into a method. Perhaps behind their objective, almost impersonal approach to the classroom there was an intense inwardness, a profound concern with what might happen to each pupil at every moment. Children, one is almost forced to conclude, can sense this inner reality behind the disguise of externals. How else are we to explain why they forgive an adult long before the adult can forgive himself for the acts of anger and cruelty he perpetrates upon them? What teacher has not had the eerie feeling that pupils are penetrating his outer words and gestures and reading off the real meaning behind them?

The sense of the miraculous, the sense of the infinite volume of life's possibilities is essential to the depth dimension of personality. Life achieves a stereoscopic effect by combining views from various perspectives into a set of deeds and demeanors we call a personality. It would be strange if straightforward analysis of overt behavior succeeded in trapping all the contrasts and nuances that give depth to the teacher and the teaching act. Perhaps that is why millions of dollars spent on isolating the traits of the successful teacher have turned up all sorts of interesting and valuable information about all sorts of things—indeed about everything except the object of the search itself.

Voluntary Segregation

On May 17, 1954, when the United States Supreme Court decreed that race-segregated schools, however equal they might be in physical equipment and personnel, were inherently unequal, these schools were finished. Little Rock, New Orleans, and other localities would achieve notoriety because of their resistance to the decision, but the ultimate shape of things was indelibly outlined.

It will take time to modify the conditioning mechanism that triggered the viscera of certain people and set off emotional explosions whenever mingling of the races in the public schools was mentioned. There will be much personal agony, just as there would be if one were forced to eat foods that one has abhorred since infancy. All the assurances of logic, all the promptings of human feeling and abstract ideas of justice will not of themselves cancel out the fright and loathing occasioned by a nervous system deaf to the arguments of reason.

Nevertheless, once the reconditioning processes do get under way, they can be counted on to set off chain reactions in a new direction. Just as poverty, dirt, and ignorance increased the fear and hatred of the Negro and deprived him of opportunities to remove them, so once educational opportunity becomes real, the ignorance, poverty, and dirt will diminish and with it the causes of fear and hatred. However, because race segregation and desegregation remain so great a moral problem in American culture, there is perhaps some danger that other types of segregation may not receive the interest they deserve. For there are many kinds of segregation.

Some are legally enforced as race segregation has been. The sexes are segregated by custom and often by law in the use of washrooms or even in the use of school facilities. In olden days segregation of diverse social classes was the rule rather than the exception, and the nobility was fenced off from lower classes by law and custom. Today some hotels try to keep out clients of certain ethnic origins, and some residential areas are virtually closed to groups with or without certain characteristics.

Many of these segregational activities can be classified as voluntary. They represent the desire of a group to be apart from other groups. Instead of expelling unwanted neighbors by legal or physical means one moves away from them. But in order to make voluntary segregation effective there must be a way of keeping the unwanted persons out of the new territory, the new club, or the new school. To be a haven and a retreat, the new nest has to be defended from incursions of those who have been left behind. So legal, physical, or economic barriers have to be erected even in voluntary *apartheid.*

Around voluntary segregation there hovers a deceptive air of moral innocence. One argues that he means no harm to anyone; he merely wishes to be left alone to pursue his values and interests in common with those who share them. Surely there can be no moral taint in such a wish since no harm accrues to the excluded persons, especially if the exclusion is achieved by leaving the field to them. After all, is one morally obligated to share everything with everyone?

The innocence is, of course, only apparent and deceives nobody—certainly not the target of the exclusion. For to withdraw is to assert the superiority of the withdrawing group and at the same time to act on a belief that this superiority precludes association with the excluded group. In any language and in any culture this is correctly interpreted as a slap in the face; only in a country dedicated to democratic ideals is it necessary to argue that it means something else.

Of all types of voluntary segregation the most strategic is educational segregation and perhaps the following example will illustrate how important and powerful this kind of segregation can be.

I knew him when he was climbing the ladder of county and state politics. Call him *X*—a typical representative of many young lawyers in small towns with a future to carve. He had been elected to small county posts, then to the State Legislature and finally appointed to a job in the municipal court, a position that left him free for legal practice and yet put him in line for a judgeship, should the reigning judge retire or die during an appropriate political administration.

Attorney *X* was a member of the middle-of-the-middle class. He attended a well-established Protestant church, was conservative in his political views, and was moderately ambitious for himself and his family. He was all these things because he was born into a family that valued these behaviors and because all the people whom he respected exhibited them. They were industrious, self-reliant, intelligent, educated, and unobstrusively religious. They competed for prestige and position according to a strict code of fair play. Boys were taught not to strike their parents, womenfolk, or anyone weaker than themselves. On the other hand, boys were expected to take part in vigorous outdoor sports, stand up to the bully, and take victory and defeat with a minimum of emotional display.

Attorney *X* did not apologize for these values. He could summon in their defense a long history of achievement by the Anglo-Saxon peoples of Europe and America. That other peoples also might have these virtues Attorney *X* did not deny, and that many Anglo-Saxons did not have them he readily admitted, for he encountered them daily in the courtroom. But he was not doctrinaire in these matters. He was not concerned with Anglo-Saxons who lacked these virtues nor with non-Anglo-Saxons who possessed them.

Races and theories were not the units out of which his life was composed. Instead, the counters in his game were his family, the families in his neighborhood, the families in his church, the families in his modest political constituency, and the families in his legal practice. The biological family as a social unit was to him the significant unit, not the nation, the race, or the individual: not the nation or the race because they contained too many different kinds of families; not the individual because Attorney *X* was greatly impressed with the shaping power of the family. Black sheep shocked and puzzled him.

His preoccupation with family life led to mildly eccentric attitudes toward the miscreants who paraded through his office. His apportionment of praise and blame was often made on how far the offender departed from the norm of his family's behavior. Joe, a man who was haled before the court every other week on charges of drunkenness and beating his wife, he regarded as only moderately culpable. Joe's wife came from a good family but had degenerated into slovenly tramphood; Attorney *X* could not forgive her for this and he tended to regard Joe as an agent of cosmic justice. On the other hand, Joe's family had a well-publicized history of drunkenness, petty larceny, and disturbing the peace by a combination of drunkenness and wife beating.

Attorney *X*, therefore, could not place the full weight of moral disapproval on Joe, who was merely running true to the form of his family.

The fortnightly appearance of Joe before the judge was further complicated by Mrs. Joe's bleary dignity in the witness box. In Joe's lower-class family and its local branches, wives were often beaten, but only in the heat of anger or in the exuberance of drunken brawls. Police were summoned by neighbors and occasionally by the enraged wives. But the wives never signed complaints against their husbands and never would be so brazen as to disclose their wounds to official scrutiny. Joe's wife, coming from a middle-class family, had no such inhibitions.

So conflicting were the loyalties aroused in Attorney *X*'s breast by Joe's encounters with the law, that the hangers-on, who give so cheerful an air to municipal buildings, looked forward to hearing Attorney *X* sputter about the moral and legal paradoxes involved. Coming from so gentle a man, the outbursts acquired force from contrast. The hangers-on naturally egged him on.

It was to be expected therefore that Attorney *X* would view his own daughter's problems in family terms, and when her schooling became a problem, it would be perceived by him as a family problem. He believed that his own immediate family was charged with the responsibility for arousing in his daughter, Millie, a corresponding enthusiasm for the values to which he, his wife, his parents, his wife's parents, and their friends were committed.

The *X*'s hometown had fair-sized minority groups, but they had been in the town for at least two generations and had distributed themselves normally on the scale from good to bad on all human dimensions. Ethnic variety as such did not bother Attorney *X* nor did religious differences. Millie's play group shifted from month to month but was generally confined to the neighborhood and public or Sunday-school mates. When Attorney *X* thought about it at all, he approved the families of the children with whom Millie associated. Now and then it did happen that Millie came home with notions about the good life that disturbed him. As a rule these ideas were quotations from a particular girl friend whose father had made a great deal of money in the contracting business. This young lady wore expensive clothes, used lipstick and nail polish at a precocious age, and spoke casually of extensive travel to expensive resorts. Millie was less candid about certain bits of sex wisdom that she picked up from her friends.

When Millie entered high school, things changed. She was a good student and a popular one. Boys paid her the usual attentions and from time to time clusters of her friends found their way to her home. Attorney *X* noted among them boys and girls belonging to families whose background he knew only too well. There were also among them offspring from families that were not in trouble with the law, but were in trouble with life itself. For example, there were the sons and daughters of day laborers who with all their work had never been able to scrape up ten dollars in savings, and who considered themselves well-off when they could reduce their funded debt to five times that amount.

Clearly these boys and girls did not embody nor were they likely to embody the good attorney's values, but to Millie they embodied a much more important set of values, those of her peers. Whatever it was that young adolescents were supposed to do, these boys and girls did well, because popularity depended on doing them well. When Millie pointed out in the increasingly frequent family arguments that "all the kids" did these things, sang these songs, visited these places, and used this slang, her father would retort that he had nothing against what young people did. Teenagers, he realized, always did things that seemed strange to their elders, but he argued that a strong sense of family values was necessary during adolescence to ensure that these values would prevail and govern the conduct of adult life.

When Millie sensed that the argument was going against her and realized that the families of some of her friends could not be the friends of her own family, she retreated to a final excuse: "Well, I'm not marrying Tony (or Jimmy or Johnny). We're just having fun."

To this her father and her mother invariably replied that they were not so sure. To them every boy who fluttered around Millie was either a prospective husband or, worse still, a potential seducer. That much of this fluttering was no more than practice and experimentation with courtship techniques they completely forgot, for like the pains of childbirth, those of adolescence in the course of time mercifully are either forgotten or transformed by sentiment into something more endurable.

Inevitably Attorney *X* and Mrs. *X* began to toy with the idea of sending Millie to a good boarding school near the women's college in which they hoped she would some day matriculate. As their hold over Millie grew more precarious, as more and more of her time was spent away from their supervision, often out of sight of any of their friends, their anxiety deepened. "A girl," Attorney *X* sagely remarked, "is not a boy."

The decision to send Millie to a private school was not an easy one; she was doing well at the high school and the thought of leaving her friends frightened and outraged her. Furthermore, there was the matter of money. A good private school would be a drain on a young and still struggling lawyer. It would mean the enlargement of the mortgage, making the "good" suit last longer, and letting the family car acquire the genteel outmodedness that only the wealthy could afford. As for Mrs. *X*, the new sacrifices would simply exacerbate those she had endured since marriage.

So although the matter was discussed, although examinations of catalogues alternated with tearful protests, nothing was really done until Millie was a sophomore in high school. The time of decision arrived one evening when she brought home as a "date" no less a personage than the captain of the football team.

He was a good-looking lad and obviously a good athlete; he wore the regalia of his time, spoke the language of his peers, and was considered quite a catch by the girls. He was not of Anglo-Saxon stock; his parents were hard working and respectable, but their social pretensions extended no further. If Tony could go to college, they would be happy to have him go. More, they would work even harder to make it possible for him to go even if the athletic scholarship did not materialize. But if he chose not to go, if he did decide to get a job moving a big trailer truck across the country, as he so often wished he could, that would be acceptable to them. Tony was headed for a lower-middle class career or perhaps an upper-lower berth on the social Pullman.

The sight of Tony in his living room somehow shocked Attorney *X*. As a son-in-law, Tony did not fit the pattern he envisaged for Millie and for himself and his wife, but he did not argue with his daughter. He knew full well that he would condemn himself out of his own mouth. Before it was over his daughter would have convicted him of snobbism, provincialism, bigotry, and being out of step with the times. So instead of arguing he marched into the local bank and made the necessary arrangements for financing Millie's attendance at boarding school by increasing the mortgage on his house.

To his banker he explained his action somewhat as follows: "This is going to cost about $2500 a year for two years. On top of that I figure another $8000 to $10,000 for four years of college. What for? Not because she'll get better schooling in her subjects and not that she needs supervision that we can't give her, although I'll appreciate that too. The girl is doing well in her studies and she's no problem at home. No, the money is an investment in her future and in my peace of mind.

"How will it work? Very simple. I am paying to build a wall around her. Inside that wall will be only the boys and girls I would like to have her spend the remainder of her life with. She will not meet boys who will not make suitable husbands nor girls with whom she cannot associate in her post-college days.

"She will marry a boy who goes to the church of our choice and votes the party of our choice, live in a house pretty much like ours but costing more, have an income that will allow them all the decencies and some of the luxuries. That's worth $15,000."

Attorney *X* was, of course, protecting a set of values by voluntary segregation. By keeping his daughter away from the Tonys of the public school, she would not have to decide whether to accept or to reject Tony, because Tony would no longer be a live option in her social decisions.

On the positive side, the new environment would condition her to prefer certain clothes, foods, modes of language usage, topics of conversation, certain kinds of music, recreation, and humor. In short, the fabric of her emotional and attitudinal life would be rewoven so as to produce a pattern that would *feel* right, so right as to make all deviation either wrong or at least of doubtful propriety.

In a small town with a heterogeneous population such a distinctive pattern is impossible to maintain. By social osmosis other patterns intrude and mingle with it. Because no one item in the intruding pattern is of crucial significance by itself, it becomes easy to compromise. Tony's facial structure in itself was unimportant; his economic role as such was not an insuperable obstacle; after all, in America this was a flexible matter. His ethnic background also was not by itself an insupportable factor. It was an ethnic group that had produced a distinguished civilization and distinguished individuals. A priori there was no reason for believing that Tony could not himself be a distinguished person. But taken in summation these differences coalesced into a way of life frighteningly different from that of Attorney *X* with the odds against a successful amalgamation fearfully large, certainly large enough not to warrant the risk involved.

And so after the summer passed and September rolled around, Millie was in boarding school. Thanksgiving was a lonely time for her and her parents, but there was not enough money for both the Thanksgiving and the Christmas homecomings. At Christmas vacation Millie was met at the railroad station by her parents. She seemed as pretty and healthy as ever.

During the holiday festivities she naturally saw a great deal of her erstwhile classmates who were still in high school, but there were also invitations from boys and girls in private schools. In a small town word gets around quickly and by means of a network of friends of the family a small subculture of private school students is maintained. Millie met Tony and the others on the street, and perhaps in Millie's heart there were pangs of nostalgia and wistful memories, but she had to admit, although her father never asked, that she felt more comfortable now with young people who could talk about the folkways and mores of their respective private schools. "Not better, mind you," she said to herself, "but more comfortable and easier, if you know what I mean."

By the end of the school year, Tony had been graduated from high school and was working on a road gang, partly to earn some money, but also to toughen up for the rigors of college football. Although Millie took a clerking job for the summer, it was so obviously a temporary engagement that it differentiated her clearly from a half dozen other high school girls who held permanent positions in the store. Her leisure time was spent with the private school crowd home for the summer or the high school boys and girls whose families were firmly integrated with the families of the private school crowd.

Millie finished school. Millie finished college. Attorney *X*, threadbare and older, with Mrs. *X*, equally threadbare and equally older, attended the ceremonies and marveled that they could have contributed so charming a daughter to the world. For truth to tell neither of them was handsome. Yet Millie was not plain; she was more than pretty. She had the assurance of superiority, which meant that she did not think in terms of superiority and inferiority at all. Her judgments about people, clothes, character, and taste had lost their relativity. Despite the iconoclasm of her professors, especially those in the social sciences, certain acts and objects felt right and others did not. Man, she had been taught, was the measure of all things, but she also knew that this did not mean each and every man indiscriminately. It was her kind of man who was properly the measure of all things.

And because she was ready to live her taste, she would rarely if ever be called upon to justify it. Those who might wish to do so would obviously be the unhappy, neurotic people who would have to be understood and forgiven.

Attorney *X* had indeed succeeded in encapsulating his daughter in an environmental cocoon—a silken cocoon out of which emerged a delightful embodiment of the value package he prized so highly. It had been expensive—impoverishingly so—but it was worth it. Now would come the final seal for the future—marriage to a fine young man who also embodied his values. A lawyer, a doctor, an engineer, an architect, or a member of some solid financial firm would march Millie from the altar and they would set up a household in one of the good suburbs. A brace of happy, handsome, and healthy children would be borne and brought up amid the wholesome amenities of suburban life, and then these children would grow up into another Millie and her masculine counterpart. The values were not only embodied but insured for generation after generation of embodiment.

But how did Millie's future turn out? Was it possible that Attorney *X*'s fling at playing God would succeed? Could Millie, freed from the protection of her cocoon, resist the assaults on her affections and fortunes by all sorts of young and uncertified men? A chance trip to the city, a handsome stranger retrieving a fallen package, Tony's triumphant return from the gridirons of the nation—any of these or a thousand other little events could upset Attorney *X*'s calculations.

Drama and perhaps a sense of cosmic justice might prompt us to wish that one of these untoward events would occur to teach Attorney *X* and those like him a lesson. But Millie did just about what her father expected her to do and she did it without coercion or family pressure. She married just the sort of man and lived in just the sort of house in just the sort of community her father had envisioned. Her children (three rather than two) were as handsome, healthy, and happy as anyone could have wished, and so far as one can make out her grandchildren will be no less so.

Was Attorney *X* justified in voluntarily segregating his daughter from the competition of value schema alien to his own? Was it good for Millie? Was it good for the young men and women from whom Millie was insulated? Was it good for the attorney and his wife?

Attorney *X* was sure he was contributing to the happiness of his daughter, but he was also taking out an insurance policy against his own distress. He was sparing Millie some rough encounters with social reality and, in effect, was marshaling the forces of his values to assure himself of a painless victory.

This moral judgment itself requires little heroism because it is irresponsible. Had Millie not come through the ordeal, would the critic have paid the price? Or would it be the misery of the *X*'s that would pay the price for the mistaken decision? Not so long ago parents were confronted with the alternatives of either allowing their children to chance contracting polio during an epidemic or removing them from the area. On the one hand, they knew that should the child contract a mild case, he would become immune; on the other hand, the disease might cripple the child for life. What would or should parents with sufficient means to flee the epidemic do?

The response to this question before the advent of the Salk vaccine was: "Where will you flee and how often can you flee?" Since the danger was everywhere at some time or another, would one be doing the child any service by trying to protect him? Would it not be better for him to take the risk and perhaps win immunity? But after the news that the Salk vaccine had been discovered but before it was available, would not the parent have been justified in doing everything possible to avoid a risk that in another year might not have to be taken at all?

In recent years voluntary school segregation has been on the rise. Prosperity put such segregation within reach of many who could not have dreamed of it a decade earlier. Independent schools of all types catering to special needs, special classes, and special values have had little difficulty in finding customers. Parents are proud of the linguisitic and sartorial hallmarks that some of these schools affix to their children, but for most fathers and mothers the primary motive is still to give their children a special advantage, intellectual or moral, in the social competition, even if this should shoot their offspring well beyond their own status.

In a culture in which the value patterns of subgroups could be maintained by social solidarity and encapsulation, resorts to special schools may have been less needed, but in a world where these protective membranes have become more and more permeable, it is only natural that parents will turn to the special school that will isolate and insulate the child as the home community cannot—a school that will supervise and teach twenty-four hours a day, whose masters and mistresses are symbols of the *class father* and *class mother* and not of the individual parents made weak by their love of the child and their fears for his future. Who can blame parents for using a handy vaccine that will protect their children and stimulate strong antibodies against the dangers of adulthood? Until the community can vaccinate everyone, is it selfish for parents to protect their children from the unvaccinated ones?

The immorality, if there be any, in such reasoning lies in its selfishness, in the narrow view that places one's own child's safety above the safety of other children who have equal claims on such well-being as the society can afford to *any* of its members. But this narrow view may be the result not only of selfishness but of a lack of enlightenment as well.

For one thing, to pursue the vaccine metaphor a bit further, not all vaccines are equally potent and none, so far as I know, is potent forever. The intruding value scheme of other groups may be too powerful for the immunity built into the child by several years of special schooling. Adult life can rarely be carried on under antiseptic circumstances.

Furthermore, new viruses seem to be emerging against which new immunities have to be sought. Not even a good private school claims to provide the panacea—the universal antibiotic or serum. We need not only a set of values firmly held, but also the reflective power to interpret their relevance in each succeeding decade, for that is about the life span of any particular interpretation of love, kindness, charity, courage in our epoch.

Love, for example, is a timeless value, but the behavior which love dictates is a temporal affair changing from year to year. The nature of man makes love a categorical imperative; only the context of action and reflection can tell us what love shall be in a given situation. To love the child before the imminence of the Salk vaccine meant one action; after its proclamation, it meant another. In the world of 1910, civic courage meant one action; in 1961 it means another, but civic courage there must always be for the good life in the good society.

The best of schools, public or independent, will try to give the pupil not only a firm commitment to the great overarching values of human life but also the scientific and practical resources to seek out and to rethink these values for daily re-enactment. These are the powerful arts of learning whereby men can continue to translate the universal truths into the diverse languages of time.

But as with diseases and vaccines, the best protection is universal immunization, not individual or group immunization. And what the better independent schools can do for the few is none too good for the public schools to accomplish for the many.

Administrators and Professors

Every professional man now and then has lost a friend to administration. A strange psychological metamorphosis sets in the very moment the announcement of the promotion is made and progresses inexorably until a new relationship emerges. Let us consider a fairly typical example.

It was a friendship circle made up of faculty colleagues at a small college. At weekly "gripe" sessions many soul-satisfying hours were spent in denouncing the ineptness of the administration. Around midnight it was patently clear to all that the administration was spineless, politically motivated, and destined for that region in the Inferno allocated by Dante to the "trimmers." Invariably the night ended with vows never to become administrators, despite any appeal.

The friendship group included the wives of the faculty members, and the substantial equality in their husbands' status made for easy social intercourse. While the wives may not have shared their spouses' opinion of administrators or administration, they were wise enough to agree that money and power were not important enough to warrant a compromise with principle and integrity. They were also wise enough not to contradict the pronouncements of their husbands.

One of the members of the friendship group, despite his honesty, ability, and forthrightness, was invited to become an administrative officer at the institution and a rather important administrative officer at that. After considerable soul searching he concluded in a surprisingly short time that the new job afforded him a wider opportunity for service to his students and colleagues and presumably to his family, God, and country. The colleagues, after the initial shock, swallowed hard, shook his hand, and organized a party to celebrate his elevation. About the first statement that he made to his friends after the first flood of congratulations subsided was: "This is not going to make any difference to our friendship," a remark that was forthwith preserved both in alcohol and the memories of his friends. How long it lived in his own memory is less certain.

For a while he continued to join his colleagues for lunch and they, in turn, continued to invite him to the weekly gatherings at one home or another. But these occasions became increasingly rare. Lunch was a time when he could meet with visiting celebrities or with committees or with other administrators. And the increasingly frequent reply: "Oh, I'm so sorry we'll be tied up," put an end to the invitations to family gatherings as well.

The administrator was uneasy about this. He was not at ease when he joined his old cronies, because he was afraid lest such gatherings be interpreted as favoritism for a particular group of faculty members. After all, he wanted to avoid the political maneuvers to which his predecessor had been prone.

The wives diagnosed the situation far more rapidly and accurately than did the husbands. The administrator's wife was, as might be expected, attending more formal functions, dressing better, and weaving new social ties. Of course, when the old group met, everyone spoke cordially to everyone else, and first names, except on the most formal of formal occasions, were still the rule, but heartiness replaced easy intimacy until in time both intimacy and ease vanished altogether.

One interesting sign of the new role of the administrator was the change in his convention pattern. As an economics professor he had attended annual and regional meetings with other members of the department. At the meetings he looked up old classmates, old friends, and men with whom he had corresponded about academic matters. There were the usual bouts of conviviality, lively enough to be remembered but not wild enough to be recalled either with great remorse or great relish.

Now, other conventions claimed his interest and presence. Administrators, he discovered, also have their sorrows and likewise share them in convention assembled. And so as his economics meetings rolled around each year, he implored his erstwhile colleagues to remember him to So-and-So from Arkansas and So-and-So from California. Whenever circumstances drew one of these men into his new administrative orbit, he pumped his hand vigorously and was genuinely delighted to see him and talk to him. Perhaps he kept him a bit longer than was strictly necessary, as if a bit afraid that luck would not soon arrange another meeting. When, as sometimes happened, certain conventions brought administrators and staff members together, he dined and joked with his fellow administrators. Presumably they too had their *convivia.*

One cannot be sure, but it did seem as if with the very same eyes the new administrator now perceived people differently. Old Joe, the groundskeeper, had always presented the image of the gnarled, rough, but kindly soul who paced himself carefully so that he never seemed idle or rushed. Old Joe, he and his colleagues had agreed on many occasions, represented the best solution to a frustrating world. Now, however, the groundskeeper, still old and stable, rough, leisurely, and wise, had acquired a new perceptible quality: that of being a budget item. Old Joe's careful pacing, seen in a different light, represented inefficiency and waste. Before he became an administrator, employees had never appeared to be "lines in a budget," had never had what Heidegger has called "the quality of being a tool" (*Zeug*). Of course, these were not the only characteristics they now had. Old Joe was still a fine human being, and Professor Longtenure too, although a plodding old duffer, was the finest of men.

Nevertheless, the image of Professor Longtenure, a plodding old duffer, fine man and all that, wavered and faded into the vision of Dr. Brighteneager, Alpha College, a young up-and-coming chap who could give the department a shot in the arm and perhaps even a reputation. This vision, one can guess, was accompanied by the shock of having been disloyal to Professor Longtenure, his fine wife, and fine children. At any rate, he was crowding the retirement age and certainly it would not be disloyal to project the vision, let us say, three and one-half years into the future. Certainly, it would not be disloyal to bring in Dr. Brighteneager for a summer session of teaching.

Melancholy as these changes may have been to the characters in the story, the more important question is: Must administrators and employees be enemies? There is, of course, a quick answer. It is "no," "of course not," "by no means." For is it not obvious that both are working for the same goal? That one needs the other? That the success of one is contingent on the success of the other? That some of one's best friends are janitors, employees, and administrators?

But is it not equally obvious that this is too easy an answer? Surely, if it were true, transition from one role to the other would not produce such pervasive and often painful consequences? Certainly the differences in power, prestige, and rewards would not be so marked. For it is only in Heaven that perfect marriages and perfect organizations are to be found. Here on earth the general good and the individual's good do conflict, now more, now less. The administrator's good is not always the good of this or that employee, although rarely is it different from that of all his employees taken collectively.

The *science* of administration quite properly concerns itself with the laws that govern the duties of administrators and employees in the abstract. It works on the only possible assumption it can make, namely, that the good of employee and administrator is one and the same. The *art* of administration consists in mitigating the conflict that in fact exists between them.

Difficult as the lot of all administrators no doubt is, to administer a staff composed of professional workers is to encounter a special kind of difficulty. Organizations employing teachers, physicians, lawyers, engineers, scientists, and clergymen on a salary basis are familiar enough, but the day may come when all industrial and business concerns may have to employ substantial numbers of professional men. When that day arrives, the head of the industrial corporation will commune more understandingly and sympathetically with the managers of hospitals and college presidents.

Professional workers have peculiar loyalty patterns. Jim, the lathe operator, has loyalties to his family, to his fellow workers, and perhaps to his union of lathe workers, but it would be odd to say that Jim had his first or indeed any loyalty to lathe operation. Should a foreman tell him to operate the machine in a way contrary to efficient lathe operation, he might remonstrate or make rude remarks, but he would be unlikely to quit his job. After all, if the foreman is stupid, that is his superior's business. Jim is selling his time to the company; if the company chooses to waste it, it is no skin off his nose. On the other hand, a physician working in a drug firm or a hospital would surprise us if he talked this way when a superior ordered him to do what he knew to be contrary to good medical practice or to medical ethics. His first loyalty is to medicine.

Caught between the demands of a given institution and his professional integrity, the professional has no doubt: the latter comes first. A business administrator expects that the good of the firm will be regarded by his employees as paramount, and generally these expectations are acknowledged as valid. A man who takes a job with the Acute Manufacturing Company is expected to work for its profit and general welfare. His personal integrity may limit what he will do for Acute, but no professional allegiances will interpose themselves to harass his superiors—unless, of course, he is a lawyer, doctor, scientist, and the like.

The loyalty to the profession or to the code of the profession is therefore an important curb on the power of the administrator, for it represents a diversion of loyalty toward another, and in this instance, superior authority. But the consequences of this relation to one's profession do not end with the frustration of the administrator when circumstances cause institutional and professional demands to clash. Paradoxically, the educational administrator is expected not only to respect the profession's demands on the worker, but he is also expected to promote, within limits, the professional growth of the individual worker at the institution's expense.

For example, what would happen if an important worker, let us say a traffic manager at General Motors, requested a leave of absence for a year to work at Ford? The possibility of such a situation is so incongruous to the practices of commercial enterprise that the idea of such a request seems strange indeed. When this same kind of request from a professor of chemistry or philosophy is received by the members of a university Board of Trustees, it is easy to see that they may not readily understand it, especially if they have been recruited from businesses where such requests are not customary. Yet any academic administrator knows that the refusal of such a request, even on grounds that the institution would be hurt by the professor's absence, would arouse indignation in the faculty.

Why? Partly because the rules of the academic game require it. More importantly, professional growth is not simply of benefit to the individual achieving it; professional growth also means growth of the profession and, more especially, of the body of knowledge and experience by virtue of which the profession makes its bid for social importance. Thus an institution devoted to the growth of knowledge would be in a peculiar situation if it refused the means of such growth to its scholars. On the contrary, the institution is supposed to nurture this growth joyfully, not grudgingly; generously, not in a niggardly fashion—the more joyful and generous in this regard, the better the institution.

Further, academic personnel tend to look on the administrator as an errand boy hired to expedite their teaching or research or whatever it is that engrosses them at the moment. The dean is not likely to be perceived as a father figure, especially by the contingent of gray beards who may well have had him in their classes and recall him as only a fair student in their speciality.

By contrast, public school superintendents, especially in smaller communities, are more likely to take on the image of the great father surrounded by flocks of fluttering female school teachers. He is an obvious source of authority and grace. They serve; he protects and provides. He fights for salary increases and new buildings and against predators who would deny the schools their sustenance. Even to a male teacher the administrator is clearly a power figure whom it is not safe to oppose or criticize unless, of course, one has a good prospect of supplanting him.

Those who wonder why the American public school teacher is so successfully denied professional status may find it instructive to look at his relation to the administrator. Public school teachers tend to behave like employees in a business. It is quite normal for them to report to work at a certain time, to check out at a certain time and to resent working after official hours. It is also quite consistent (although morally it presents some problems) for them to organize into unions in order to achieve bargaining rights against their employers. Indeed, they would be innocent of the ways of a corporate society if they did not try to do so.*

Occasionally, a public school executive honestly tries to share his power with teachers. He consults them on policy and even invites them to share in the making of it. Curricula are at this moment being revised in hundreds of school systems by committees of teachers. Thousands of teachers are taking courses for the purpose of "professional" improvement. These activities signify an attempt to make teachers behave like lawyers, doctors, engineers, scholars, and to cease behaving like the hourly-wage employees of the Acute Manufacturing Company.

To many teachers these responsibilities are just so much extra work (which, of course, they are). To others it signifies laziness on the administrator's part. Why does he not do it himself? He gets paid to do it. Still others accept it as "part of the job" and do it as part of that job. Still others suspect the administrator of maneuvering them into carrying out his wishes under the guise of making them believe that it is their

* This topic is discussed in the essay "Teachers, Strikes, and the Art of Payment."

decisions that are being executed. Who knows and who can say how often these attitudes and suspicions are justified? How often are administrators taught in courses on administration that such social engineering and manipulation are legitimate devices of good administration?

One may take it as a rule of thumb that whenever democracy comes from the top the people at the bottom are probably not ready for it; when professionalization is urged by the administrator his personnel are probably not ready for it. Some things, unfortunately, are better wrested from the authorities than conferred by them.

When school personnel are professionalized they will not have to be urged to shape curricula, make policy, and exercise leadership. Instead, the administration will be hard put to prevent them doing so. Nor will the executive be a father figure, because their primary loyalty will be neither to him nor to the institution. In short, professionalized workers never quite accept the employee status in fact, even though their contracts use the word. A doctor does not work *for* a hospital or a clinic, he works *at* a hospital; a professor does not work *for* Harvard or Purdue, he works *at* these institutions. Should a physician say that he works "for" Acute Manufacturing Co., we are quick to translate it to "at" lest perchance he really means what he has said.

For these reasons professionalized personnel find it difficult to organize themselves for bargaining purposes, although they do organize for other purposes—not always laudable ones. It is especially awkward for them to withhold their services as a bargaining threat if, in order to coerce their employers, they have to hurt clients, patients, and pupils, and not merely customers and stockholders. A union that will not strike is not much of a union; a profession that will strike lacks certain characteristics of what may be called a "learned, humane profession."

A moot case is provided by the Newspaper Guild, a union made up of workers who regard themselves and are generally regarded by the public as professionals. Yet newspaper writing lacks certain conventional marks of a "learned, humane profession": a body of theory to serve as a basis for professional training, recognized requirements for practice of the profession, and licenses to practice. Perhaps the fourth estate is still an appropriate designation for this calling. In any event, a strike by this guild is seen by the public, first of all, as an injury to the owners of the newspaper and, second, as a public inconvenience. There is no feeling that in refusing to gather and publish news the reporter is damaging the health or welfare of any particular client or patient.

Yet it is a safe guess that an administrator would rather deal with well-organized employees than with unorganized professionals. Organized workers want group benefits. If a worker falls within a given classification, he gets the benefits. The classification is based on such incontrovertible criteria as age, length of service, years of formal training, and the like. Subjective criteria such as effort, loyalty to the company, going beyond the call of duty may measure merit in the eyes of the employer but not necessarily in the eyes of fellow workers. The worker is willing to give up a claim to special consideration for his superior merit in return for the superior bargaining power which uniform pay schedules give to his group. The employer, for his part, in return for a little administrative peace, is willing to give up the dream of each employee straining to the utmost to achieve greater rewards for himself.

After all, a deal is a deal. One gives a little, gets a little, but when it is finished, one has regularized one's relations with all the employees at a stroke. With professional employees, especially if they are not well organized for collective bargaining, there can be no deals and no peace. Teachers, quite properly and with the weight of all kinds of economic evidence to back them up, want more money. But no two teachers, especially at the more advanced levels of schooling, perform precisely the same tasks in the same way or with the same people. The quality of their academic degrees, the amount of self-improvement, the effort and zeal, and a half dozen other variables loom large to each teacher, and any salary schedule is bound to seem unfair if it is uniform. The objective criteria that prevent controversy are precisely the least important to them. Genuinely collective bargaining comes hard to them—the uneasiness being in proportion to the non-collective character of their work.

Worse still, professional workers are in principle opposed to any group judgment of merit, because any grouping cancels out the individuality of the worker's contribution. Thus it comes to this: either each worker judges his own merit, or the administrator judges each worker's merit. No sizable institution, to my knowledge, has dared try the first alternative and no administrator in his right mind would want to undertake the second.

To the administrator this would be a veritable hell, because it calls upon him to make judgments of a Solomon, not once or twice, but hundreds of times each year. And because money and rank are the only means of payment currently recognized as legal tender in the academic profession, the number of unsatisfied academic employees would bulk large in comparison with the satisfied ones.

Rank—now there is a pretty problem for the administrator. The logical justification of rank derives from a hierarchy of tasks that requires differentiation of function and authority. Military, industrial, and some religious organizations have, no doubt, put some sense into the chains of command and titles appropriate to each link in the chain. Academic ranks may also have had some rationale at one time, but whatever it was is now difficult to discern. A commercial firm was recently engaged to make a study of salary readjustments for state employees. With prison guards, road construction gangs, and even state hospital workers, the problems of job description and grading were not insuperable. A given job called for certain duties, stipulated so much formal education and experience, and that was about it. But when the firm tried to navigate the apparently mild waters of the hierarchy of professors, associate professors, assistant professors, instructors, and assistants of various orders, the investigative craft with all its scientific gear foundered.

What does a professor do? He teaches, sometimes does research, and maybe writes articles and books. What does an associate professor do? He teaches, sometimes does research, and maybe writes articles and books. What does an assistant professor do? He does what the associate and the full professor do. What does an instructor do? He teaches more and writes less. Do professors supervise associate professors? Not necessarily. Are they older than the occupants of lower rank? Not necessarily. Do they work longer hours? Not necessarily.

One question read: "How many employees do you supervise?" Office managers, foremen, bureau directors, dietitians, purchasing agents, accountants, and prison wardens had no difficulty answering this question. But it created dismay among the professors. Most of them did not supervise anybody and they did not view with customary respect those who did. How could salaries, they wanted to know, be determined by such silly questions?

After a while the investigators threw up their hands, threw away their carefully prepared forms, and left it to a committee of the faculty to establish the appropriate wage differentials for what to them seemed to be distinctions without discernible differences. There are differences, to be sure, and there is a sense in which they are real, although not readily discernible and not easily justified in this or that institution. But they are not functional differences and thus they bedevil the administrator, if he himself is not a participant in the academic mystique.

Or take another area. Academic personnel are sensitive about infringements on freedom that other employees take in stride. The citizenry interpret this as a confession of secret yearnings to break rules and laws with impunity. They shrug their shoulders and say, "I don't know why these damned professors balk at taking oaths. I don't mind taking them." What they forget is that their work does not depend on freedom whereas the professor's does. The moment his allegiance is pre-empted by anything other than his profession, his professional life is limited in principle, however little in fact. The academic man has no small difficulty in making clear just why his case is not like that of the plumber's or that of the electrical engineer's. But it is different. When an electrical engineer, for example, takes an oath to be loyal to the Constitution of the United States, what does he promise with respect to the way he designs electrical circuits or machines? Nothing. He promises not to spy on the United States, sell its secrets to foreign nations, work for a foreign power, and conspire to foment attacks against the United States. But the practice of electrical engineering is the same, whether in the hands of a loyal or a disloyal engineer.

When a professor or a clergyman or a lawyer and sometimes even a doctor takes an oath *as a professional man,* what does he promise? He promises what the engineer did, that is, not to commit treasonable acts or to contribute to such acts. No citizen is averse to such an oath—especially if he plans to break it. But the professional man is expected to promise more than this. He is expected to promise that he will not think, utter, or write anything that may challenge accepted beliefs or practices. But what if his very professional life consists in examining beliefs and practices, and what if his oath to the profession is a solemn promise to challenge wherever his convictions lead?

A professional's profession—if it is a learned one—depends on a freedom of thought in a way that other workers' does not. And the more closely a man's work touches the fundamental values of life, the more he needs the freedom and the more onerous the oath is. A sociologist needs freedom more than the physicist, a philosopher more than a physician or a biologist, and both more than the professor of accounting.

To be sure, many instances of violation of "academic freedom" are nothing of the sort. They are rather violations of a professor's rights as a citizen to say and do things while occupying the position of a professor at a school. If he chooses to wear a long beard, be a vegetarian, have many wives, and the like, he will have to suffer the consequences, legal and otherwise. But these punishments do not interfere with his right to investigate and publish in his field. That they may get him out of a job is quite likely, but this is another matter. Any criminal act may get a man out of his job by depositing him in jail. As for noncriminal acts, the consequences vary from institution to institution. In some schools there is a wide tolerance of deviation, and in others, not. One should inquire into these matters, if they are important, before taking a post at a school.

Wise institutions and those confident of their status can tolerate considerable eccentricity in their professors and students. A university that gets the wind up every time a laboratory assistant incurs the wrath of the more sensitive citizens in the community is merely inviting interference into its affairs. Indeed so delicate and precious is the right to intellectual freedom in a school that its preservation is worth considerable sacrifice elsewhere. That is why perhaps the academic community will rally to the defense of a colleague whose lack of wisdom and taste abuses the freedom they are defending; occasional idiocy and bad taste are, on the whole, a small price to pay for the principle itself.

All of this does not, however, make the life of an academic administrator a happy one. But there are compensations. If professionalized personnel do not contribute much to the administrator's father-ruler cravings, neither do they demand that he behave like an omnipotent and omniscient father. They do not depend on him directly to carry on their own work or achieve their growth. If they do not admire him simply *because* he is an administrator, they will respect him if he is a good one and be grateful *for* him, if not *to* him. If they look on him as a means to their own professional goals, they are also willing to be means to his plans—provided they accept the plans. There is no watching the clock and no insistence on holidays and overtime pay. There are no days or hours that they will not work when their professional obligations demand it.

If one were to pick out the one feature of corporate life that contributes most to whatever animosity may obtain between academic personnel at the professional level and the administration, it would be, I believe, the apparatus of administration—or red tape.

One need not belabor the *absolute necessity of procedures* in any large-scale enterprise. Anyone with a smidge of common sense can see with half an eye that there would be chaos without the slips, forms, blanks, applications, referrals, channels, and so forth.

Almost inevitably the administrator comes to personify in the minds of the staff the vast system of procedures that are interposed between the agent and his goal. He is accused of using the machinery to protect himself from importunate personnel. He can use it to avoid making decisions. He can use it to delay action until a project withers from inaction.

Without fail, it seems that whenever an administrative official is asked what he thinks about something interesting that has just happened at his institution he replies, "I have not yet received a report on this matter and therefore can make no comment at this time." The event can be anything—a fire, embezzlement of funds, the suicide of the chairman of the board, or the rebellious remarks of the football coach. No administrator knows anything until he receives an official report from the right official.

Paradoxically, it is not the young employees who are most impatient with red tape but rather those who still remember the times when matters were less complex. The young cheerfully accept institutional procedures as they accept other aspects of life to which they have experienced no alternatives.

It becomes a sign of good administration to camouflage procedural apparatus or to conceal it from the victims and beneficiaries alike. In one university, visiting faculty during a summer session were harried continually by the demands of the administrative machinery. It was easier to get married than to cash a check, and to get a classroom changed was a project of the first magnitude. Throughout the session the major-domos of physical plant made instruction impossible by the cutting of grass and carrying on repairs to roads and buildings. Although there were empty classrooms in other more quiet parts of the campus, no one was able to discover the administrative formula to remedy the situation. At this same institution a visiting professor, who by a clerical error was incorporated into its retirement system, had a devil of a time retrieving his involuntary contributions to it and relieving himself of benefits promised by it.

Yet in another institution with machinery no less complicated a few intelligent secretaries made the visiting faculty feel that the administrative labyrinths were put there just for convenience and comfort—which, as a matter of fact, they probably were. They accomplished this by such simple expedients as preparing in one packet all the forms to be signed, the keys he would need, a parking permit, and identity cards without which the visitor would be virtually helpless. Taken separately, these technicalities are trivia; collectively, they add up to a first-rate nuisance.

In perhaps the unhappiest of all situations is the institution where the administrative machinery is not quite adequate to its size and complexity. Usually this happens in schools that grow rather slowly. In one such school, for example, it was possible to communicate with every member of the faculty by walking down the corridor of one building. Students were interviewed in corridors, on the grounds, wherever they were met. There was a minimum of forms, reports, records, and procedural arrangements and everything went on tolerably well. Occasionally there were sins of omission and duplication because of slips in the communication "system," but they could be corrected with informal dispatch.

Gradually the student body and faculty increased in size and without anyone realizing it a mild sort of chaos set in. Committee meetings were called but half of the members failed to appear. Students left school and were not missed for weeks. Guidance broke down; irritation increased until the inevitable occurred: new administrative machinery was introduced and everyone was irritated anew, but for different reasons.

In Freudian psychology we have become acquainted with the notions of sadism and masochism. Sadism refers to a tendency to enjoy the inflicting of pain; masochism to the enjoyment of suffering pain. Sadism is represented in administration by a tendency to give personnel responsibility without adequate power to discharge it, and masochism is the tendency of personnel to acquiesce in the arrangement.

A favorite form of sadism is to call in a department head or a principal and tell him that he is to be responsible for the policy of his school or department. Henceforth he is to make decisions, give orders, reorganize, hire, fire, move, spend, and allot as he sees fit. There is, of course, a hitch. All orders, firings, hirings, purchases, and shifts will have to be approved by the superintendent or dean, Board of Trustees, and three different bureaus in the state government. And, of course, money will have to be appropriated before it is spent and, further, it will have to be spent according to the rules and regulations of the three boards, the purchasing bureau, and the statutes of the state.

This is administrative sadism because only someone who enjoyed harassing people would talk this kind of nonsense and only those who enjoyed being hurt would listen to it.

What gives plausibility to this sadism is the fact that for months on end—perhaps years—the upper layers of administration do not overrule the lower ones. After a while a dean, for example, takes for granted that the President and Board of Trustees will automatically approve his recommendations. He achieves a sense of power through use and finally comes to believe he really has it. But he finds to his sorrow that, given a controversial appointment or purchase, he can be cut down from an eagle to a sparrow with humiliating speed. Clipped once, he thereafter gets his permission *before* he uses his power and after a while the upper echelons of authority shake their heads sadly and conclude that Dean Y will never make the grade, being "altogether too timid and afraid to assume responsibility." Dean Y has become a bureaucrat, an expert in defense.

Some administrators need repeated clippings and burnings before they acquire caution; others learn faster—probably a matter of intelligence. But once the lesson is thoroughly learned, the trained bureaucrat divides his time between performing strictly defined tasks according to the rules of the establishment and making sure that he cannot be blamed should anything go wrong.

A well-run bureau develops procedures for defense of the bureaucrat. They consist primarily of insisting that everyone put everything into writing. He gives due notice of what he is about to do; receives written permission to do it; reports that he has done it and sees to it that his superiors receive notice that it has been done. He protects his front, side, and rear. If anything does go wrong he can, by assembling his memoranda, prove that he had warned against the action in the first place; that he performed it under proper authorization; that he had taken all the prescribed precautions, made all the required checks, notified all the parties concerned; and finally, that he had not said, done, or caused to be said or done whatever it was that contributed to the misadventure.

As his duties become more complicated, the bureaucrat has to employ sub-bureaucrats to write his memoranda, and each of these in turn is compelled to protect himself against all possibility of blame. Each therefore has to instate into the order of things his own memoranda about his work in connection with writing memoranda. As a result of this system of wheels within wheels, a sort of insurance policy against blame is created; the network of forms and rules prevents procedural lapses from occurring. All misfortunes are then to be charged to Someone Else whose identity must forever remain secret, unless perchance he failed to write a memorandum, or what is even less forgivable, failed to keep a copy of it.

Schools, colleges, and universities are not exempt from these devices of management of men and things. To rebel against red tape is to endanger the whole enterprise, an act that even a neophyte in administration can demonstrate to be psychologically childish and morally bad. How much of the energy and time of an institution should go into turning the wheels of its machinery? It is something like using up so much of an automobile's power to help in steering, shifting gears, and braking, that little is left to propel the vehicle. There comes a time when the results no longer justify the elaboration of the machinery. If instruction is the prime activity of schooling, then everything else is overhead; we reach the point of absurdity when the instruction is tailored to maintain the overhead.

It is little wonder that educational enterprises, as they grow large and complicated, look to other corporate structures for devices of management. Inevitably management and administration emerge as specialties in their own right and become professionalized in their own right. And with this development the paradox and the dialectic are complete. We now have professional administrators whose first loyalty is to their profession, that is, to its laws and principles, and only secondarily to the particular enterprise they are administering. So it may not be odd at all in the future to hear of a president of a corporation or a university resigning rather than violating the principles of sound administration, and it may not be odd in the future for General Motors to allow some of its administrators to work at Ford for the greater growth and glory of the administrator and the profession of administration. With this development, the barriers between the professional administrator and professional worker may collapse in their common devotion to professionalism.

Until this development is completed the elevation of any professional to administrative status is bound to occasion a twinge of regret on both sides, for it does signify a change of loyalties. To a devoted professional, any object of loyalty other than his own profession is a false god, and defection from the old object smacks of betrayal and idolatry.

The professor, lawyer, or doctor who steps up into administration, protesting that this will not make a difference in his relations to his colleagues, protests too much. He may see them every day, but he will never again see them from the same perspective. That he is rising to a higher estate and better things does not alter the fact that he is leaving; his colleagues would be sad even if his leaving elevated him to the order of angels.

LAYMEN AND EXPERTS

Brookline is a prosperous and venerable suburb of Boston. Its population consists of a thin layer of Boston Brahmins, a heavy layer of upper-middle-class professional and business men, an even larger slice of middle-class entrepreneurs, and, of course, the usual contingent of semi-skilled and unskilled workers. Because Brookline is noted for its wealth and enlightenment, one tends to overlook such poverty as it may still harbor. Despite its size (over 50,000) and wealth, it disdains the title of "city" and as a "town" remains loyal to the town meeting, the purest of American democratic forms, as its basic legislative authority. There are those who say that Brookline's destiny in history is to serve as a constant rebuke to the evils of the big city, Boston, where, incidentally, most Brookliners earn their incomes. Brookline's cleanliness, purity of government, devotion to the higher values, and municipal efficiency are supposed to show the world what democracy could amount to if it were operated by the right kind of people. Brookline's school system reflects the unique syndrome of its civic virtues: it is expensive but not extravagant; modern but intent on solid intellectual outcomes; and experimental in an unobtrusive way.

In 1944 the Brookline schools began to teach manuscript writing (printing) on the recommendation of a special handwriting committee. The intent was to remedy the notorious illegibility of juvenile handwriting. According to newspaper accounts, objections to manuscript writing became vocal in 1953. A mother is said to have complained that her son had been unable to read a postcard she sent him from Hawaii. Other mothers complained that their children could not read a written grocery list and similar notations.

Matters simmered along. A parents' research committee was formed. Meetings with the superintendent were held, petitions were circulated, and opinion polls of teachers and parents were taken. Studies were initiated. A bill was introduced into the state legislature to require the teaching of cursive (ordinary) writing. Most of the difficulty was over meetings. The parents' group, according to newspaper accounts, was invited to attend an executive session of the School Committee but declined, demanding an open meeting instead. The School Committee stated that the parents had been invited to another meeting and failed to make an appearance. The committee scheduled public meetings for May and October and a four-hour conference in November of the year 1953.

It is interesting to note how well the mechanics of protest and reform had developed in this literate and progressive community. The small group, the meetings with the authorities, the bringing together of large numbers of "interested" persons, the rallying of experts, the collecting of data for the buttressing of argument—these are intricate mechanisms calling for skill in organization and a good deal of telephoning, writing, and ringing of doorbells. Part of the mechanics might be called the rituals or procedures of fair play; part might be called the rituals of democratic action. Each side was careful about procedural correctness lest the other side cry "foul."

Finally the drama approached a climax. The School Committee voted to continue manuscript writing, but to make a course in cursive writing elective at the seventh-grade level. The gauntlet down, the opponents had recourse to the ballot box, putting up candidates for the School Committee in the fall of 1954. Committee members who supported manuscript writing were decisively victorious.

Many curriculum controversies involve freedom of speech or the firing of a teacher for political reasons. Others represent economic interests in conflict. In such cases the arguments are no more than verbal smoke screens. The teacher or book being attacked or defended is only a symbol of deeper conflicts; indeed, the school itself is converted into a symbolic arena; the real battleground lies outside the school. Not so, I believe, in the handwriting case. Aside from a preference for the "old" writing, which might be interpreted as a form of conservatism, one is hard put to find secret political, social, and economic struggles of which the controversy could be a symbol. It was an educational tempest in an educational teapot.

As a rule, parents do not become irritated with their schools because they are unhappy with the curriculum, the organization, or even the financing of the system. A parent is more likely to become annoyed or even infuriated by the circumstance that he cannot find a parking place while waiting for a child to come out of school; or that a child is allowed to roll merrily in the snow during recess and then sit around in wet clothes for the remainder of the session; or that one's offspring is not treated "fairly" by a particular teacher; or that the vacation periods of the school do not conform with the vacation plans of the parents; or that a son or daughter cannot enter a certain college because the wrong subjects were taken or the right subjects indifferently completed. Such happenings lead to sputterings, complaints to the principal, the school board, and an occasional letter to the editor. Conversely, many parents are enthusiastic about a school or a teacher for reasons no more general or profound than those that occasion the complaints.

It has been my privilege to address many parent-teacher groups, but the number of times that matters of high educational policy were challenged by parents is so small that I cannot clearly recollect even one of them. When policy is questioned, it is usually because the shoe pinches in a particular spot. A parent who thinks the high school should, on principle, pay more attention to academic work and stop fooling around with courses on dating and recreation will, if pressed, admit that his evidence comes from his own family. His child is not doing well enough in high school to get into college but is doing quite well, perhaps too well, socially. On the other hand, a parent who deplores the high school's emphasis on academic accomplishment is more often than not sincerely disturbed either over a child's emotional maladjustment or his academic inadequacy, or both. It is only natural that parents should look to the school for the kind of help they need for *their* children. But it is also natural that they should make the complaint in the name of a principle or policy—at least to start with.

We act in response to some desire or aversion, but we justify the act by something other than our desire. Somehow we need to believe that what we did was also the right thing to do. When a child is asked why he gobbled up the pie that was to serve as dessert, the child may answer that he was hungry. Mother may accept this as an explanation as to what moved him to eat it, but it does not satisfy her that this made it right for him to eat the *pie,* especially if there were other food items available. The child knew that the pie was for dessert and that consuming the dessert at 3:30 p.m. was not the right thing to do. The culprit lacks an authorizing principle for his conduct.

Authority is the name we give to power exercised in the name of some higher power, as when a policeman exercises power in the name of the law, and the legislature in the name of the people. In whose name do the people act? In the name of the Common Good. But what is in any particular instance the Common Good? Is it what this man, that man, or a majority of them want? Or is it what a majority believe is the best alternative in the situation? Just as hunger explains but does not justify eating the dessert, so the wants of the voters explain but do not of themselves justify their acts. In either example a moral principle is needed for justification and such a principle is often expressed in the following form: We ought to act in behalf of the Common Good and to determine that good by knowledge rather than wishes. Knowledge, accordingly, together with intent to act rightly becomes the source of moral authority from which all more restricted authority derives.

In a highly developed technological culture the knowledge needed to ascertain the Common Good, or indeed any good, is technical and specialized; the expert becomes the source and measure of the best available knowledge; he is a moral instrumentality and therefore a source of moral authority.

Sometimes the available knowledge is not adequate, as for example, our knowledge about the causes of cancer and mental breakdowns. Sometimes the experts disagree, as they do in the danger of fall-out from hydrogen bombs, or the best methods of rearing children. Nevertheless, if there are experts, we ought to take their knowledge into account in making our decisions, and if we must decide between them when they disagree, it again ought to be in terms of the best available knowledge. But what kind of knowledge?

In education the problem is complicated by the circumstance that school policy necessarily gets mixed up with other areas of life. Where is the expert to harmonize the varieties of values that each one of us is trying to realize? To be sure, handwriting experts know a great deal about handwriting, but do they have a proper appreciation of the need of a mother in Hawaii to communicate with her son via postcards?

It would seem, therefore, that when a question about school matters is before us, we must separate out, first of all, that part of the question which is technical. What ought to be taught, when it ought to be taught, to whom, and how—these are all technical questions; at least they become technical questions once we know the goals education is to serve. In matters of health our goal is clear; we want to stay well. Concerning the kind of life we regard as good there may be a fundamental agreement, but on the surface men not only disagree, they disagree and insist that certain ways of life are bad and endanger the Common Good. Which value scheme the schools espouse is, therefore, not a matter of indifference to the competing groups; live and let live is not a principle to which they are willing to resort in educational policy. The educational expert can tell us that if we are aiming for certain kinds of value experience, if there are certain qualities of personality that we desire in our children, if we are committed to some life style, then this and this will have to be done *educationally*. He cannot, however, prescribe the goals of life. Furthermore, if a certain life style requires other than educational experience, for example, medical care, nutrition, housing, or peace, the education expert reaches the limits of his usefulness rather quickly. He can write an educational prescription; whether the citizen can get it filled; whether he wants to get it filled, or ought to get it filled is not part of the prescription.

Even if, ideally, the citizen could get the best expert opinion on every phase of his problem, he would still have to adjudicate among the different phases himself. The knowledge needed for such adjudication is wisdom. There is a sense, therefore, in which we are at the mercy of the experts and shall be increasingly so, but in a deeper sense the salvation, if there be salvation, lies within each one of us alone—in our own moral integrity and wisdom. Integrity requires that we always act with the best knowledge available; wisdom requires that we achieve a knowledge and appreciation of the good life which order our values according to their perspective.

In the handwriting controversy the experts wrote an educational prescription. That is why the objectors were careful to invoke the support of research, that is, expert testimony. In Brookline a non-scientific, non-objective posture is not respectable and one might go so far as to say it is immoral. Once experts were confronted with counter-experts, the issue was no longer a technical one and controversy had to ascend to the level of life-styles and values. The School Committee and ultimately the electorate had to decide which experts to trust and which to support. In this instance the authority of the school officers was sustained by the people, but it is to be noted that this authority could be properly challenged only when the expertness of the experts was called into question. Further, the decision of the people was not an "expert" decision but a declaration of confidence in one set of experts. This did not make them or the people more expert in educational procedures.

One may object that we have complicated matters unduly: that after all, since the people pay for the schools, they own them and can command how their money shall be spent. If one used this argument in building a bridge or removing an appendix, the absurdity of the argument would become patent. No ethical engineering firm is going to erect a bridge that will collapse merely because whoever was paying the bill wanted it built that way, and no ethical surgeon in performing an operation will accede to the desires of the patient merely because he is paying the bill.

The relation between the public and the expert is not that of an owner to a commodity nor, strictly speaking, that of an employer to an employee. While the public can do what it likes with its school buildings, it cannot do what it wills with the services of its experts. This is so because the expert's will is so tied to the rules of his expertness that morally neither he nor his "employer" can act to contravene them. Each expert has, so to speak, a domain of ethical relevance in which his professional conscience is authoritative. At most, the employer can fire experts who will not carry out his wishes.

From time to time the reluctance of professional educators to be advised by laymen on educational matters has been severely criticized, but I believe this is due to a lack of discrimination on both sides as to where the professional domain of ethical relevance begins and ends. A layman's views on the propriety of reading *Brave New World* in high school literature classes is educationally irrelevant, but an educator's attempt to abolish capitalism is no less so.

When it comes to apportioning its resources among diverse goals; when priorities among life values have to be established, we cannot resort to experts. It is not that we reject the expert; there is no expert to reject because this is not a technical matter. We are reduced to exercising wisdom. We expect that the expert will put his expertise at our disposal.

Only as laymen, as citizens, as human beings, do we have wisdom. Our choice is right if we have fulfilled the first claim of the moral law:

that we act in accordance with the best knowledge available with regard to all the value dimensions of our situation. Beyond this there is no further duty—at least in this world, and from it there is no appeal because at any given moment the wisdom of the community is what it is.

Educators are experts in education but probably no more and no less wise than the layman in other matters. This is the professional view and casts the schoolman in a role analogous to that of the doctor or lawyer. He prescribes the right thing to do educationally, will refuse to do the wrong thing, but just what within the code of his profession he will be permitted to do depends on the layman. In other words, he does not claim the moral knowledge wherewith to decide for the people just how educational values shall be assessed in relation to the other goods and miseries of life.

The clear-cut separation between wisdom and expertness is logically justifiable and practically indispensable. Specialization and expertness go together, but we pay a price for it. There comes a time when the maintenance of health requires an array of specialists beyond the financial resources of the patient. This may be good science and good medicine, but if it puts adequate treatment beyond the reach of the patient, this is not an unmixed blessing. But an even more important consideration is that amidst the concern of the eye specialist, the liver specialist, the bone specialist, and other specialists, the patient's health may well drop from view altogether.

At this stage of specialization there arises a need for mediating specialties and specialists. This is a hybrid sort of calling that interposes a concern for the entire patient or the entire enterprise—whether it be medical, educational, political—between the specialists and the layman. By repeatedly taking the broader view within a given domain of thought or action, one becomes a specialist in taking the broader view. Thus, while a specialist in generality sounds like a contradiction in terms, he comes into being as a necessary counterweight to over-specialization.

In education such a mediating role has been assumed by the discipline of philosophy of education. The term is perhaps unduly exalted, conjuring up the visions of Socrates, Plato, and other great teachers. At a much more modest level, it makes one think of venerable schoolmasters reminiscing about their experiences and making sound observations about schools and life.

The philosopher of education does not presume to approximate Plato's Guardians; he is not that wise. His own vision of the good life does not have the authority either of universal knowledge or of universal assent. Neither does he have the expertise of the doctor, the engineer, or even of the educational specialist in testing or curriculum. Nor does he simply combine specialization and wisdom.

He is a specialist in that he studies the philosophical dimension of educational problems. In the Brookline case, for example, he could explore the relations of the handwriting controversy to the other educational values involved, and he could assay the weights to be attached to the judgments and prescriptions of the various specialists involved. More important than this, however, would be his awareness of the value schemes of the community and how they related to the problem at hand; he could supply perspective.

Like all specialists who draw their knowledge from many fields, philosophers of education are only as good as the knowledge they master. Expertness in educational theory and certain aspects of philosophy are indispensable. While the hope that superficial acquaintance with Fields A and B will, by some alchemy, result in deep knowledge in Field AB is vain, expertness in A and B may with effort and luck result in expertness in AB.

It has been said that philosophy criticizes, analyzes, synthesizes, and systematizes whatever it touches. A philosophical approach to education operates in the same ways. It examines educational theory and practice for logical consistency and linguistic clarity. It helps in this way to keep education up to date and decently sophisticated. In its analytical-synthesizing operation, the philosophy of education tries to define the elements of an educational enterprise more sharply while exploring their interrelations assiduously. In systematizing, the philosopher of education tries to arrange in some coherent order beliefs about educational policy, aims, curriculum, organization, and the methods of teaching and learning. Done properly, a philosophy of education is, therefore, not to be confused with a credo in which are listed eight or eighteen articles of faith concerning democracy and the good life. There is a vast difference between the generalist who is general because there are no specialists in his field and the generalist who comes into existence precisely because there are too many specialties.

Trained specialists in the philosophy of education can affect the educational enterprise in at least two ways: first, by teaching prospective educational workers how to structure their problems philosophically, and second, by serving as consultants to school systems, legislative committees, and other bodies which are studying educational problems. In neither role are they sources of ready-made solutions. They are rather sources of clarification of meaning and perspective—and education, as everyone knows, can do with a good deal of both.

Paradox & Promise

Teachers, Strikes, and the Art of Payment

In the first book of the *Republic,* Socrates makes the following points:

> Each art gives us a particular good and not merely a general one—medicine, for example, gives us health; navigation safety at sea, and so on.
>
> And the art of payment has the special function of giving pay: but we do not confuse this with other arts.
>
> And when the artist is benefited by receiving pay the advantage is gained by an additional use of the art of pay, which is not the art professed by him.
>
> Then the pay is not derived by the several artists from their respective arts. But the truth is, that while the art of medicine gives health, and the art of the builder builds a house, another art attends them which is the art of pay.*

There are three modes of payment, Socrates notes, to induce men to hold public office, that is, to exercise the art of government. These are money, honor, or a penalty for refusing, the penalty being to be governed by bad men. Socrates could have extended the argument to all the arts. Persons are persuaded to practice them by money, prestige, or the fear that lesser men will not practice them well enough for the social good.

This little aside in the *Republic* has not received much attention. The book discusses issues of far greater weight. Indeed, the comments quoted are merely part of the logical footwork by which Socrates befuddles Thrasymachus and which does not carry the conviction of the arguments in the later books of the *Republic.*

* From p. 346A and *passim* in the Benjamin Jowett translation of Plato's *Republic.* Reprinted by permission of the Oxford University Press.

An aside or not, it touches a sensitive nerve. Is there an art of payment? Do societies cultivate such an art? Does it have a body of principles upon which it can be based? What are these principles? Is there an art of payment comparable to the arts of building, navigation, medicine, or government? In what sense do we have individuals or groups of them practicing the art of paying people for what they do?

In one sense all of us practice the art of payment whenever we spend money for anything, ascribe status to a calling, or whenever we invite men to imagine what their art would come to should they allow meaner talents to displace them.

There is not in our culture, nor was there in Athens, so far as I know, a class of price fixers, whose prime concern is to adjudicate what payment shall be given to whom and for what. There is no group of people who are by profession paymasters.

On the other hand, experience in two wars and, in between the wars, with totalitarian governments, indicates that Plato's aside may have been prescient. A controlled economy guided by some goal or ideology develops an art of payment, because it adjudicates the money value of every component in the economic enterprise in terms of national defense, political ambitions, manifest destiny, or whatever other notion might captivate the minds of the ruling classes. One can in such circumstances imagine a set of men devoting themselves exclusively to the art of payment, the three kinds of payment Plato mentioned: money, honor, and the threat of a given art being practiced by inferior men.

A neat example of this kind of manipulation is afforded by the way theoretical scientists had greatness thrust upon them by the governmental plans of Russia and subsequently by all nations with national fears or ambitions that involved space missiles. Russia used money, prestige, and, one supposes, the threat that, "If you don't, someone else will," to elevate the position of scientific inquiry on the Russian value ladder. We did the same, but more subtly.

It was once held by classic economic theory that, ideally, the price of all goods and services should be fixed by the "laws" of supply and demand operating in a free market, in which presumably nobody would artificially withhold supplies or stimulate nonproductive and immoral demands. That is to say, in an ideal market, nobody, for example, would withhold food in order to raise its price, and nobody would stimulate a demand for opium, cosmetics with faked claims, and new clothing and automobiles merely for the sake of keeping up with fashion. Plato himself in the *Republic* half ironically sketches out an ideal economic system in which only necessary pleasures and needs constitute the normal demand, and the work of artisans devoted to the practice of the necessary arts constitutes the normal supply. Exchange is then simply a mechanism for distribution. A luxurious society, he conceded, would require a more complicated economy.

This ideal has served as a principle that could, in turn, serve as a norm for the art of payment. To everyone according to need and from everyone according to ability is only a Marxian translation of this ideal. but it is to be noted that in both the Platonic and Communist versions, it is not simply *any* demand and *any* supply that are to interact, but purified demands and purified supplies; both contained a norm of human nature and its needs. Even classical Adam Smith economics in the minds of the Enlightened philosophers carried a proviso that the brutal battle for survival be carried on under rules that would prevent the strong from using their strength to make the market unfree. Or in plainer language, responsible thinkers never quite plumped for an impersonal catch-as-catch-can economic struggle for survival. By a free fight they always meant a fair fight.

Unfortunately, at no time in history were men born into a system that had not already been somewhat corrupted. The fight was no longer fair. Not only had some combatants become stronger than others, but their strength had enabled them to change the rules of the game in their favor—at least, so the social theorists always explained. Thus in any going society the market was already rigged to favor some activities and some classes, and the government as a referee was also under the control of the more successful riggers. Hence the notion of the *really* free market is used as an ideal wherewith to rebuke the injustices that have grown up. The government, since it can be seized by any group that becomes sufficiently powerful, becomes a prize instrument for changing the rules of the economic game and is therefore the target of all revolutions violent or parliamentary.

The normal state of affairs, therefore, is to have individuals or groups complaining that the going system of payments is unfair, corrupt, or at the least incompatible with the goals it purports to espouse. Some examples of each type of complaint follow.

First, there are the plain and simple poor who are always to be with us, we are told. They are the people who cannot earn enough to satisfy their bodily needs. They never get enough food, warmth, light, shelter, and rest to achieve satiety. To argue that what they do to earn a living deserves no more by the rules of economic exchange does not alter the fact that they are not sated with the pleasures and comforts they naturally crave. Some say that any society which permits this to happen has neither a just style of payment nor an efficient one. Quite possibly they are right because it does seem well within our productive and distributive power to send our millions to bed well-fed, warm, and healthy. But in a more important sense the lusts of the body are self-limiting and satiation reduces their force.

Little men can be cruel when lust and gluttony possess them, but there is a limit to how far one can hurt others in catering to one's desires for food, sex, and brawling. But when money or honor, as such, are the goads to action, there is no satiety; instead there is perpetual and powerful dissatisfaction. Larger and larger numbers of people have to be drawn in as fuel to feed the fires of desire, so the evil wrought is on a large scale. Common sense and good will may relieve the deprivations of the poor, but nothing can remove the obsessions and compulsions of power- and prestige-hungry men. Hence every Utopia is, sooner or later, trapped into promising a change in human nature as a solution to the world's ills. The art of payment would seem to consist, therefore, of schemes for circumventing or limiting unlimited desires for money, power, and glory so that there will be enough goods and services to keep the economic enterprise on an even keel.

Another kind of dissatisfaction with the art of payment is somewhat more fundamental than the unhappiness of those who simply want more money, power, and prestige than they happen to have. The more basic discontent is rooted in the question: Why does one kind of social service receive higher rewards than another? Why, for example, does a popular professional entertainer receive enormous returns in money and prestige as compared with the successful professor or the successful preacher? Why does the producer of a gadget reap a fortune while the discoverer of the principle that makes the gadget possible dies unhonored and poor?

School teachers, especially public school teachers, have in recent years become a symbol of a society that has something cockeyed about its style of payment. The discrepancy between the social importance of the teacher's services and the rewards for rendering them is so great that the man with even average sensibilities is seized by the feeling that something ought to be done about it—something ought to be done to change the style of payment. But who can bring about this change?

The people by changing their values could do so; so one might begin by persuading them to alter their value perspectives. Another method is to bring pressure on legislative bodies to change the style of payment. For example, 30,000 school teachers could by persuading their own families marshal 150,000 votes. In a close state election these might be decisive, and a committee of the teachers could negotiate with the political parties on a realistic basis. Finally, teachers could exert pressure by withholding or threatening to withhold their services collectively by a strike and thus goad the people into forcing an acquiescence to their demands.

Oddly enough, each of these corporate methods of correcting the style of payment is frowned upon by the American public. Why, it is difficult to say, because so often they acknowledge the cause as just and the means as effective.

Perhaps it is an instinctive resistance to pressure as such; perhaps it is a deep inchoate guilt feeling that they have been derelict in their duty to the teacher and thus to their children and to their own ideals. Perhaps a more fundamental clue to the anomalous feelings of the public toward teachers is to be found in the relation of a humane profession to the social order, for it is with respect to the humane professions that the public is most queasy when resort is had to collective political and economic pressure, especially the latter. The thought of servants of the public health and safety—teachers, physicians, clergymen, lawyers, and public employees—striking to enforce even the most just demands shocks many citizens who sympathize with labor unions and acknowledge the right to strike as a weapon in collective bargaining.

By a humane profession or art I mean one that ministers directly to the critical needs of the person. By "critical" I mean those needs the satisfaction of which not only makes life possible but eminently satisfactory and the denial of which endangers either life itself or the good life. It is important to note that these ministrations are applied directly to the individual. The superintendent of a hospital ministers to health and so does the commissioner of sewers, but not directly as does the physician.

Furthermore, humane services, insofar as they are professional, are based upon science or sciences that are not easily learned or not learned at all by simple apprenticeship. Most important of all, humane services concern matters of greatest importance to the individual: his health or life, freedom, happiness, or salvation. Medicine, law, and the ministry have, accordingly, been the prime exemplars of the humane professions because they combine all of these characteristics. Some professions are learned but do not serve individuals directly, e.g., engineering, architecture, scholarship, or scientific research as such. Other vocations, like nursing and embalming, serve individuals directly but are not learned in the meaning used above; they are crafts rather than professions. Still other callings serve our convenience directly but do not directly affect the deeper and more critical values of life, for example, barbers and gas station attendants.

Teaching is a borderline case. At one end of the scale it can be regarded as a craft; at the other it approaches scholarship, but somewhere between the two is the teacher as a genuinely humane professional, that is, one who ministers directly to individuals with respect to their personal development on the basis of skill and knowledge that comprise a distinctive discipline. Public school teachers are especially vulnerable to the ambiguity of their status because with respect to their payment and promotion they are regarded as craftsmen, but with respect to their responsibility, they are regarded as professionals. Only on the importance of their work is there clear agreement.

The relationship between the professional man and his client in the humane professions makes it difficult for him to resort to any of the usual corporate methods of correcting the style of payment for his services, especially the method of striking—for the following reasons.

1. Intrinsic values are not comparable to each other or indeed with any other values. What, for example, is the value of a doctor's services when a child is seriously ill? How does one measure it? With a commodity these questions can be answered by putting it on the market. With some services the question can be answered in a somewhat different but no less definite way. What is it worth to have one's car lubricated? One's suit pressed? One's tooth filled? One's income tax made out? Here one weighs the inconvenience of doing these things oneself, or suffering the consequences of leaving them undone, against a price and makes a choice. In time we standardize the price of the service in terms of time used, materials needed, cost of training, scarcity, and other economic factors. Performance of these services has also been standardized so that the practitioner faces no momentous options. Indeed, the refusal of these

practitioners to take responsibility beyond that of doing the customary things in the standard situation may well be the straw that breaks the back of the technological camel. The culture will break down not for lack of inventive genius or scientific fruitfulness, but rather because of the multitude of appliances that cannot be kept in repair by impersonal service men.

But to the parent of a sick child the value of saving the life of the child or even of rescuing it from agony is incommensurable with any commodity. What would the parent give? He would give everything. But how much is everything? It varies from individual to individual. We say therefore that this is an intrinsic value and not relative to any other, not even to another life.

2. When we try to think of the services of the humane professions in terms of exchange of equivalents, we run into another oddity. The lawyer who gets justice for his client has lost nothing, but the beneficiary gains everything. The lawyer has not depleted his store of learning or skill; if anything, he has augmented it. If he has lost anything it is his time, but for what else could he have used his time? He could have devoted it to making money, but then our problem disappears. Or he could have used it to serve a richer client whose "everything" was far greater than the "everything" of a very poor one. But for either client he can only secure justice. How then can he choose between them, except on nonprofessional grounds or even perhaps on contraprofessional grounds?

3. What does it mean to owe the benefactor "everything"—everything one now has, or everything one will ever have? Clearly this is a debt that one can never pay, but what sort of debt is such an obligation? We call it a debt of gratitude, which is never discharged and is yet discharged completely whenever the beneficiary is genuinely grateful—even for a moment.

But this is merely a way of speaking. One cannot discharge a debt of gratitude; one can only furnish tokens of it accompanied by such expressions as: "I know that this doesn't make up for what you did, but it will show you how we feel." Such tokens of gratitude are properly called gratuities because they issue from the gratitude of the beneficiary and are not fees for services rendered or goods purchased. The benefactor has no moral claim on such gratitude, but the beneficiary has a moral obligation as a person to feel it and, if possible, to give tokens of it.

This relation of benefactor to beneficiary is one into which all of us fall now and then. We help the stranded motorist get on his way; we help a neighbor simply because he needs help. We do not expect a *quid pro quo* or a reward, but we are annoyed if there is no gratitude, even though we have no right to demand it. The humane professional, however, is in this relation vocationally. The important point is that this is quite different from the customer-seller relation or the employer-employee relation where exchange is the heart of the relation and gratitude has no place.

No one in his right mind would expect a storekeeper to give a customer a suit of clothes because the customer needed one, and no one expects a tradesman or a craftsman to contribute his services free of charge. Yet when one is sick, afoul of the law, or in jeopardy of damnation we expect the appropriate professional to perform his duties regardless of the probability of payment. Much to the chagrin of doctors and lawyers and perhaps of clergymen also, some of their beneficiaries abuse the proper relation between professional and client. They expect doctors' bills to be waived if they cannot pay them, or to wait until more exigent creditors are satisfied. And the practice of charging according to the resources of the client aids and abets this abuse of the relation, for if what is involved is the exchange of a commodity, then on what possible grounds should the rich patient be expected to pay more for an appendectomy than the poor patient? But if the relation is one of gratitude, it makes sense to expect that the rich man's tokens will be greater than that of the poor man, who often can give no more than a verbal token, notoriously the cheapest kind.

Consequently, the attempt of the humane professions to charge standard fees may succeed, but will also be resented, and we may now guess at the reason: the resistance of man to the transformation of an intrinsic value of life to an impersonal commodity of exchange. In other words, when doctors and lawyers try to work out a rational art of payment for their services they collide with primordial intuitions that the nature of things is otherwise. That clients cannot articulate this intuition is beside the point.

Whether the common man or the professional is right is perhaps indeterminable, but one can ask of the professional that he not insist on eating his cake and having it too. He must not expect the prestige payment accorded the public benefactor, as the intercessionary of men with unseen powers in times of crisis, and at the same time exact a money payment for his services as if they were a commodity on the free market. He cannot detach the service from himself and expect a personal relation to himself because of the service.

All of the aforegoing does not solve the problem of paying the professional, especially the practitioner of the humane professions. It merely tries to locate the difficulties that confront one in trying to solve it. For clearly, if they cannot be recompensed properly by the free market, their human needs for material goods and services must be provided and indeed guaranteed by some other means.

One of these devices is political pressure and the other I shall call economic threat. The political solution is to persuade those who have political power to provide for the needs of the professional in a manner that the profession believes appropriate.

I see no clear-cut principles by which one can gauge such a standard of living, save perhaps the principle that it be high enough to keep people coming into the profession and to keep them practicing it at a high level of competence. But at best these standards are loose and variable. At worst they are beside the point, because the demand for a standard of living is not made in the name of one's profession. One does not say, "I need a high-priced automobile and television set to be a good doctor," and certainly one need not say that children must attend an expensive college in order for their father to practice medicine or law. No, these demands are made by the professional as a man living in a given society and having many roles to fill that have little to do with the practice of his profession. But because he cannot trade his services on a free market, he has to resort to other means for making sure that he and his family enjoy the kind of life he regards as good. I see no way in which one group can legislate for another what this life shall be.

It is quite in order, therefore, for professionals to unite in political combinations for political action to secure material or social benefits that they cannot otherwise secure, just as they have a right to take political actions to insure the proper practice of their profession. Physicians are the proper judges of what good medical practice is, but only the political authority can adjudicate how much power to enforce their convictions it will permit the profession to have. And if the people deny them their plea for proper payment, what then?

At this point it has been argued that the only recourse left is a strike or the withholding of services in order to persuade the body politic to accede to one's requests. Doctors by not treating their patients, teachers by refusing to teach their classes, lawyers by refusing to represent their clients, and presumably clergymen by refusing to administer rites will bring the body politic to its knees. The whole history of the labor union movement is cited as an example of how effective this device is, and further, that this is the only realistic way of dealing with a body politic that will pay no more than it is forced to for anything.

It is at this point that teaching and teachers are caught in a quandary. Is it morally permissible for them to withhold their services in order to enforce economic or even professional demands, demands that in the long run might benefit the pupils whom they temporarily refuse to teach?

The question seems clearer if a physician attending an individual patient is used as an example. It would be unthinkable for such a doctor to refuse to treat a sick man on the grounds that the American Medical Association had called a strike for some worthy cause. The case is more problematical when the physician is permanently on the staff of some hospital, when his salary comes from an institution rather than from an individual patient directly. Yet the withholding of his services from a patient raises the same problem as if he were treating a private patient. Who gets hurt by the withholding? Has the victim a choice in the situation? Is he responsible for it? Can he remedy it? We can ask the same questions during a teacher's strike. This is not a doctrinaire matter; it can be reduced to concrete moral transactions. If the withholding hurts someone for nothing he has done and perhaps for nothing that he can at the moment remedy, it is tantamount to inflicting pain and suffering on the innocent, and this would be hard to justify on any moral principles. Even if it were clear that this suffering is for a greater good, one would still have the burden of proving beyond any reasonable doubt that this is the only alternative, and that the good will be so great that the freedom of the victim not to choose the ulterior good is less worthy than the expected result.

Suppose the patient is told: "I shall not treat you now, but if you perish, be consoled that future generations will get better medical care because of your sacrifice." The patient might retort: "I do not choose to make this sacrifice. I was not consulted about it. I doubt that it will have the effect you predict, and I can think of other ways to achieve the same result."

The moral principle to which the withholding of services as a means of collective bargaining is most repugnant is that which forbids the willful injuring of the innocent for a good other than their own. Without some injury or threat thereof the strike as a weapon loses its edge. Therefore the injury to be morally defensible must be directed against those who had a voice in creating the evil situation; who can by their own action negotiate with the strikers; who can, therefore, act as moral agents. When such conditions obtain in schools, hospitals, and law courts strikes lose their moral awkwardness. It is not easy to conceive of such situations, but they are not inconceivable. For example, physicians hired by insurance companies to examine prospective insurees could strike for better pay or working conditions or some other goal without thereby inflicting injury on their patients, largely because their relation to the prospective policyholder is not that of physician to patient. Likewise, junior law clerks could strike against their firm if this did not entail ceasing service to a client in the throes of a law suit. That is why other callings that are, without doubt, professional by all customary standards, can strike without moral onus. Engineers, architects, newspapermen, and even scholars can withhold their services without injuring an innocent client directly and immediately.

The fact that such strikes threaten a possible client indirectly rather than an actual client directly makes a big difference in the moral situation. The possible patient and client may wish, as a citizen, to bring pressure to bear on the appropriate bargaining powers to consider the claims of the strikers. Thus, it is not immoral to tell the public that if the pay scale of school teachers or doctors or professors falls below a certain level, there will be too few entries into these callings to meet the need for their services. But is it morally justifiable to confront a sick patient or a pupil with the alternatives: either *they* raise my pay, or I stop teaching or treating *you* tomorrow at noon?

The problem of strikes and teachers is complicated by the fact that they are in most instances public employees, and in some states strikes by governmental employees are forbidden by law. The only factor that gives plausibility to the general indignation at such a strike is the moral one, namely, that concern for the public's safety, health, or convenience is superior to the worker's demands. But if the argument is to be made on moral grounds, then legal arguments are not especially relevant. If it is a moral matter, the public and its representatives also have their share of the responsibility for a work stoppage. There is no principle by which one could a priori predict that the public will always be right in these conflicts of interest.

Of course there is one form of withholding services that eludes some of the onus of the strike in the humane professions. It is to refuse to enter the profession or to stay in it. When this is a reasonable and possible alternative, the act is a protest against a society's style of payment which is not only effective but also morally justified—up to a point. One would be less likely to condone it during an epidemic, a war, or in other unusual circumstances when the impact of the withholding on individual clients is virtually assured and immediate. But these factors will have to be weighed by the individual before he can assess the moral praise or blame to be attached to his withdrawal. Often the sacrifice a man undergoes in such a withdrawal itself guarantees that his motives are just and directed toward the public good.

The reason for saying "up to a point" when judging the moral rightness of not entering a profession or withdrawing from it as a protest against the society's style of payment can be indicated by an example. Suppose a college student who is interested in teaching or medicine or law, who has the ability to enter the profession, and who recognizes the need for his services, makes up his mind, on economic grounds, to enter a more lucrative calling. If this is his sole determinant it smacks of callous selfishness that is difficult to defend, for he himself will want others to provide for him the very services that he has refused to render.

The professional callings, especially the humane ones, cannot recruit and operate solely on economic grounds and cannot reward their practitioners solely by money. The profession becomes, as Abraham Flexner pointed out, a brotherhood dedicated not only to serving its clients but also to the knowledge and skill that make up the "rites," if you like, of the profession. If people are not motivated by a desire to be of the brotherhood, if they do not see themselves as servants of a body of knowledge and ideals greater than their own individual retirement plans, they have no business in a profession of this sort. They confuse or even equate the practice of the profession with the art of payment. They then treat their patients and clients as means merely; such treatment is a moral betrayal as well as a professional one.

However, none of these strictures apply, as has already been noted, to professionals banding together to augment their political power. Indeed this becomes almost a duty, inasmuch as no other way is open to them to protect the profession, secure sufficient replacements, keep the quality of training and service high, and improve the quality of the service. This the public, on its own, cannot do and will not do. The teacher who meekly hopes that the grateful public will give larger tokens of gratitude is a mean soul, hoping that gratitude will turn into something else, yet being afraid to demand it.

Lobbies in state capitals, lobbies in Washington, lobbies in the United Nations are legitimate means for a profession to educate the public and to persuade its duly elected and appointed officers to do their duty to the profession and the public. That these can be misused, as they sometimes have been, is regrettably true, but the public is rarely fooled in these matters. When the demi-gods sink their feet too far in the clay, the worshipers know it, for suddenly the gods seem less tall; their gaze is no longer up and far away, but rather down and close, too close.

The patient owes the benefactor *gratitude,* but the social order is not so related to the profession. Society owes the profession a scale of *payment* adequate to its proper functioning. Political persuasion is a means of reminding the body politic of this social fact and of keeping its value perspectives straight.

Those Godless Schools

What is one to think of a constitution that in one and the same amendment, the very first as a matter of fact, says that "Congress shall make no law respecting an establishment of religion, or prohibiting the exercise thereof"?

Most of the controversy respecting church and state in this country has swirled around the "establishment" part, especially as to what it shall mean in terms of aid to religious schools or religious instruction. But what if one is to argue—as many have—that in forbidding state aid to religious instruction the state has in effect made a law that limits religion even if it does not legally prohibit the exercise thereof?

And how are we to decide when aid is indeed aid? When is aid to a citizen not aid to his religious institution? Any money he may earn, for example, could be donated by him for the support of his church. Should church members therefore be prevented from holding jobs? Why do states refrain from taxing religious organizations? Is not this a very substantial form of aid?

In this, as in so many other matters, the noble paradox makes our national constitution a fascinating document. With fine disregard for logical niceties, like a well-bred dowager with not the slightest doubt as to what is good, proper and right, it simply announces the ideals which Americans must serve. Consistency, the hobgoblin of little minds, is not one of the Constitution's faults.

Of course it can be argued that, read properly, the Constitution of the United States of America is a set of probems, not a set of answers. So construed, it is not surprising to have the Constitution pose the problem: How does one combine in a single community religious diversity and religious freedom? How can each man be permitted to worship as he sees fit without one sect overpowering another, or, perhaps, all the others? How can each man or group be allowed to grow to full strength and yet be prevented from inhibiting the strength or exploiting the weakness of others?

Strength and dominance in the natural order of things go together. By limiting the citizens' strength, the state can more easily preserve its own power. Despots operate on this maxim without moral inhibitions. Only an idealistic democracy would seriously exhort its citizens to become as strong as possible and in the same breath announce that they are not to use this strength against each other.

When our democratic commitment therefore calls for religious peace amid religious rivalry, the schools adopt a posture appropriate to the occasion. Since the situation is awkward, the posture is no less so.

This awkwardness is caused by the often noted fact that the American mood is secular rather than religious. Not only do we lust after the comforts of the flesh, but our energies as a nation are channeled toward material progress, improved technology, in short, what William F. Ogburn called the "material culture." This materialism is not confined to the United States; it characterizes the whole epoch. Americans are simply better at it than most other nations.

Interest in theological matters is about on a par with interest in archeology; religious categories are not prominent in American speech and presumably not in thought either. There is, on the contrary, determination to keep religious thinking out of business, politics, and other areas of life. One would surmise, therefore, that the importance of religious differences would by now have atrophied, let us say, to that of differences in birthplace. The difference between being an Iowan and a Nebraskan, for example, is hardly an earth-shaking matter and even those notorious deviants, Vermonters, are regarded nowadays as merely eccentric.

However, if one were to consider religious differences to be a matter of general unconcern to most Americans he would be mistaken. While the average American may not be intensely religious; while his church membership and attendance may fall short in many respects, religious differences are not unimportant to him. They are likely to be important, however, only as signs of other differences. When a merchant discovers that his religious affiliation draws or repels customers he becomes acutely conscious of religious differences; when a boy cannot gain admittance to a college because of his religious affiliation, or when his admittance is facilitated by it, he becomes acutely aware of such differences. If and when political success depends on the solidarity of religious groups, it would be unrealistic for office seekers to ignore these differences, however much they may publicly inveigh against bigotry. The rules of the game prescribe one as rigorously as the other.

We combine in our national life a formal, legal indifference to differences in religion with a social, political, and economic preoccupation with such differences. If this conflict were not already sufficiently embarrassing, there is another to exacerbate it. How is one to reconcile the following two positions? (1) Religious diversity is important, so important that we must guarantee by law the freedom to be religiously different from others. (2) A man's religious affiliation is to be ignored in politics, economics, education, and in all ascription of status and distribution of power. If religion is *not* important in these areas of life, in heaven's name, one might reasonably ask, in what sense *is* it important?

It is a familiar observation that we Americans have officially a highly puritanical attitude toward sex and yet are intensely preoccupied with it. The psychoanalysts tell us that we are preoccupied with it because we are afraid of it and have guilt feelings about it. Perhaps they would say something similar about our attitudes toward religion. We protest too much about intolerance, about the irrelevance of religious affiliation. It may betoken a deep preoccupation with precisely the differences we are so vehemently denying.

The problem of religion in the schools cannot be solved as long as our attitudes toward it are so ambivalent; yet it is difficult to foresee the time when they will become less so. For there are, it seems, only two really promising solutions. One is to restrict religion to a Sunday or Saturday activity that is disconnected from other activities. This is a radical solution that takes the difference or, better, the irrelevance theory seriously. A man's religious life would really make no difference to his profession, his economic behavior, whom he would marry, and how he would vote.

Conceivably a man's religious affiliation could be reduced to a biographical idiosyncrasy, interesting but not important, certainly nowhere nearly so important as age, education, and membership in golf clubs. That this has to some extent occurred is beyond question. Business, especially big business, and national defense simply cannot afford to reject talent and customers on any count. Given sufficient desperation, religious equality could, one might suppose, be achieved in this way.

This solution has been entertained and urged by many thinkers—of whom Voltaire and Marx were the most outspoken—who honestly believe religion an unnecessary and mischievous vestige of human ignorance and superstition. It is expressed as anticlericalism or as a protest against the political power of churches, but deep down there is the conviction that the world in general and the United States in particular would be better off if the ideals of democracy were the object of veneration rather than the God of Abraham, Isaac, Jacob, and Jesus.

Through their positions on college faculties and their influence on textbook writers for all levels of schooling, such thinkers have accelerated secularization. The great authority and prestige of the natural sciences and the lesser glory of the social sciences also militate for this emphasis, even though no direct attack on religion is made and no derogatory opinions about it are expressed. It is not, to take a metaphor from hotel keeping, that one denies religion a room; one merely announces that all the rooms are already occupied, presumably by guests with prior reservations.

Another form of this solution is to make religion a matter of taste. One may thus argue that just as there is no accounting for or disputing about tastes in art or foods, so is a man's religion his own business. If he chooses to associate with people who share his tastes in religion as others socialize their interests in Vivaldi's music or the foods of the Near East, then that, too, is his own business.

Either form of this solution—displacement of religious activity by social service and science, or its reduction to a hobby—would, of course, be a solution of the problem by elimination. Why this solution is so stubbornly resisted in every culture—in the face of Russia's "hard sell" as well as our own gentler persuaders—is itself a vexing question. Psychologists and sociologists have names for it; folkways, mores, cultural lags, Oedipus complexes, or just plain ignorance. But explanations do not alter facts. And the fact is that, despite drifts here and shifts there, religion is for most people not merely a convention or a hobby. It is, one suspects, far more potent a factor in their lives than their speech or even their overt acts would indicate.

Another approach is more devious and subtle. It consists of fusing the religious values with the other values to produce a new compound with qualities distinctively its own. Sex provides a convenient illustration. Add the aesthetic dimension to sex and the whole business takes on a quality that neither the aesthetic nor the sexual had by itself. As an animal function, sex is a violent spasm, calling, as it were, for a suspension of humanity. Art can, however, make even this activity human. It transforms crude feeling by presenting the sex object and the sexual quest in such a way that they seem beautiful, noble, exalted, while not losing their seductive power. And if allowance be made for exaggeration, Oscar Wilde's dictum that Nature imitates art may apply here, and it may be said that human sex life is shaped more by art and religion than *vice versa*.

Similar transformations ensue when other value ingredients are added to the sex experience. Add the intellectual element and sex becomes a phenomenon to be studied, described, explained, and argued about. The moral perspective suffuses the physiological spasm with duties, claims, and obligations. The religious approach transports it from Paradise to Hell and back again to Heaven. Indeed, by the time all of these ingredients have finished their work, the simple physiological sex transaction is so changed and obscured that according to the Freudians and the Kinsey researchers it is exceedingly hard to find—especially among educated, middle income groups.

So religious experience—the experience of prayer, communion, adoration, worship—furnishes a distinctive dimension of life, the dimension of the holy and sacred. It can in the economy of the well-educated man suffuse and combine with other dimensions to give all of life its distinctive flavor. Life can be holy just as it can be beautiful, true, morally righteous, socially productive, and technologically efficient.

The difference between the two approaches to religion is that in the first we add something religious to life which remains apart from the other ingredients. It can be enjoyed or valued for itself and it adds something to the variety and richness of life, just as a stew with six vegetables is more variegated than one with three. It is like adding music, for example, to a dinner party. It can be enjoyed if one chooses to listen to it and it adds to the cost of the dinner, but it does not change our attitude toward the food or our dinner companions.

The second approach is more ambitious; it would, if it succeeded, make all of life religious. Albert Schweitzer and Mahatma Gandhi are popular modern examples of God-intoxicated men whose lives exhibit religious conceptions and disciplines. Now if one picks examples from this level, sectarian differences seem to recede into the background. The unity of mankind rather than denominational partisanship seem to be the prime object of their preoccupation.

But both approaches—the additive and the suffusing—can produce preoccupation with sectarianism as well. That a man keeps his religion apart from his business and his politics does not mean that religious differences are unimportant to him. He is not immune to fanaticism. Indeed our very best fanatics are those men who can ignore the incompatibility of their religious beliefs with the principles that guide their own actions.

Well below the Gandhi, Schweitzer, or St. Francis level are those religious souls whose daily lives are laced with prayers, invocations, and rites. Firm in the belief that the ritualistic utterances and acts are in and of themselves able to keep them from harm and to promote their every venture, these people are far from belittling sectarian differences. In other words, the fact that religion permeates life does not make one immune to fanaticism either.

Neither approach, therefore, is a sure guarantee against religious sectarianism, for neither can guarantee that these differences will be considered unimportant. The anticlericalists who hope to solve the problem of religion by reducing it to a personal idiosyncrasy on one hand, or by diffusing it into nonsectarian saintliness on the other, are probably convincing only to themselves. For the bulk of mankind, religion and sectarianism are inseparable. That some men can transcend sectarianism and live on a plane where all men are children of one God is true, but it does not mean that this plane can be reached without stepping on the lower rungs of the ladder, the rungs of a particular creed, dogma, and ritual.

The truth of the matter seems to hinge on whether religious experience—the experience of communication with the Divine—needs a specific god story, a specific ritual; whether it needs a specific set of clergymen to teach and interpret the god story, administer the ritual, and preserve the church as a social institution to perform these tasks generation after generation.

Those who are impelled to say "no" to these questions had better be sure that they are not the victims of forgetfulness. The man who believes that he can communicate with God in the forest, under a starry sky, or on the ocean forgets that from the moment of his birth certain notions and images of God, Nature, and Man were fed to him as were the nutrients that ensured the growth of his body. Just as mature muscles make him forget his puny infancy, so does his developed mind forget where its ideas originated. Just as without a tradition of science we cannot think about atoms, so without an organized religious tradition, we cannot think about God or sin or salvation. Perhaps the totally untutored man can stand in dumb awe of the vastness of nature, but that is no more the equivalent of religious experience than wonder is the equivalent of science and philosophy.

Therefore some kind of god story, telling how the Divine established relations with man, what he expects of men, and the ways by which they can reap his rewards and avoid his punishments, is essential. This story duly elaborated enables the religious person to interpret whatever happens in terms of God's will, God's plans, and God's injunctions to man.

But the story in itself is not enough. There must also be ways of communicating with God, ways of atoning for offenses against Him, ways of interceding for those who cannot make their own appeal to Him. We call these ways of behaving rites and sacraments, and it is a primitive group indeed that is without a special corps of people who are authorized experts in these matters.

The first sign of an emancipated mind is the discovery that the ritual really does not accomplish what it purports to bring about. This emancipation from magic is a heady discovery, and in the attendant excitement it is easy to conclude falsely that religion is made up of "empty" ritual. This is a little bit like discovering that words are not the things they stand for and forthwith dismissing language as an "empty" ritual. Just as language can summon up actions and feelings, so can rituals, for they re-enact what they stand for in a kind of dramatic shorthand. Rituals are empty only when they no longer summon up what they represent.

Rites and rituals make the invisible visible; they help us to imagine what is difficult to imagine. The presence of the vested clergyman at the wedding ceremony makes it easier to imagine and feel the sanctification of a new relationship between a man and woman, just as the funeral rites help one to imagine and believe that a biological fact has been transmuted by a spiritual meaning. For this is what the religious experience is all about: translating the facts of life into the language and imagery of the holy and the sacred. Or, if you like, it is the humanizing of the facts of life by making them imaginable as divinely touched, as the objects of a divine concern.

That some individuals can do this with little help from the church is probably true; that many can is probably false. And if this transmuting of fact into meaning is important to the community, what is more natural and inevitable than that it should foster and maintain an institution designed for this purpose?

The rites, the language, the music, the place, the very smell of worship, countlessly re-experienced from childhood on, shape the feelings and imagery of the worshiper. This is religious training, stocking the individual with images, thoughts, words, gestures, and attitudes. Even more important is that it provides nearly the same stock of images, thoughts, and words to all the members of the congregation.

What might religious experience be without such a common store of symbols, ideals, ideas, and images? Vague yearnings, spasmodic gesturings, inchoate mumblings might all be sincere symptoms of the religious experience, but no individual could ever see his own emotions reflected in those of others, and he could not even be sure that today's twitchings had any relation to those of yesterday. What man cannot communize and objectify he cannot believe, whether it be in science or art or religion.

In order that religious experience be objectified and thus communized it must first be shaped, given form and name. Learning the vocabulary of religious experience through story, rite, and practice can be called religious training, because the pupil is shaped from the outside. He is shaped not against his will, perhaps, but certainly not because he willed to be shaped.

With this vocabulary the pupil can some day aspire to religious education, when the rite and deed reveal the spiritual processes which they symbolize. Religious experience, like all other kind of experience, can by study and knowledge be made more subtle, more consistent, richer, and more mature. But without training such aspirations are vain.

And now comes an army of troubles. Realistic advocates of religious education, knowing full well that without religious training in creed and rite nothing "higher" will accrue, insist that the schools aid and abet, if not conduct, such training. But because creed and rite are precisely what sects disagree about, such training in or by the school seems practically or legally impossible.

Now it might be asked why sects must have different rituals and why one could not be invented that all sects could use. If each ritual is simply another way of getting to the same God and the same set of moral rules, why insist on the minutiae of the sacramental procedures, the form of prayer, the language of prayer, and the vestments of the clergy?

There may be no answer, but it is educationally advisable to consider the possibilities. The god story and the ritual resemble a drama or play with plots, actors, lines to be read and sung, and gestures to be enacted. Nevertheless, they are not a story and a play, at least not in the religious experience. Theaters are not churches, and churches, if churchmen are wise, will not become theaters.

In a theater only the most unsophisticated yokel forgets that what goes on on the stage is make-believe. The spectators maintain what the aestheticians call "psychical distance" between what they see and themselves; but in church one is not asked to make believe. A Christian is asked to *believe* that Christ was born, lived, and was crucified, and not merely to *make believe* that this was so. One does not begin a god story with "Once upon a time"; rather one says "In the beginning" or "It came to pass."

Religion calls for a strange blend of literal and imaginative thinking. One is asked to believe, for example, that certain events occurred in Palestine at a certain time and in a certain place. Moses struck a rock, went up to Mt. Sinai; Christ was born, crucified, and rose from the dead. These are descriptions of events, but they are not ordinary events, for presumably they signified more than met the eye. Their miraculous nature indicated that a fact had been transmuted into a meaning. That the event really occurred as described, the religionist is called on to believe, but what it meant he has to imagine and recreate in his own spirit before he can believe it. If one lets go the beliefs, religion evaporates into myth; if one lets go the imagination, religion becomes superstition.

Because everything in religion rests on a fact in history, a fact that transmuted all subsequent facts into meaning, what "happened" has to be particular. It must have happened to "real" persons at "real" times and in "real" places. Once a group has its god story, to change it is fatal, for it is part of the god story that the group involved did not invent it, but rather lived through it. To ask all sects to abandon their peculiarities and to unite in a general creed or common prayer is to misunderstand the nature of religion. One can, if he is sensitive and thoughtful, be graduated from a particular set of meanings suggested by ritual and story to more general meanings, but not by changing the story or ritual itself.

Seen in this way the problem of religious education in the schools becomes either absurdly simple or impossible. It is simple if one divides the task into two parts: religious training in the home or in the place of worship or both, and religious knowledge, or rather knowledge about religion, in the schools. Knowledge about religion, like all other knowledge, is universal, not sectarian. The problem of finding competent teachers is real but no more so than finding competent teachers in any field; religious history is no more controversial than any other kind, and the theologies of the various sects are as teachable as are the various philosophies. As for the familiar objections that teachers, being frail human beings, will have biases in these matters, in what areas are they free from biases?

That this simple solution gets nowhere in practice is explained not by the difficulty of teaching *about* religion in the schools but rather by the difficulty of providing religious training outside of it.

Religious training, alone, makes religion sectarian and important. As sectarian it is divisive and a danger to the American dream, precisely because by itself it leads people to order the other departments of their lives not so much by the spirit of their faith as by membership in it. Thus if there is successful religious training in the home and in the religious organization, the public school will willy-nilly have to go in seriously for religious education to protect sects from each other and all of us from disintegration of our society into sectarian camps.

If, on the other hand, the church and home do not succeed in giving religious training, religious experience will degenerate into amorphous superstition. Church membership will divide people into economic and political blocs, not on the basis of differences in belief, but merely on accidents of birth. This may already be happening in our country.

And so it would seem that those who cry out against the godless schools are barking up the wrong tree. The school cannot give religious training, and if the home and church cannot do so, the school has nothing on which to build religious education.

What then is one to make of the cryptic saying of the Founding Fathers in the Constitution? Perhaps something like this: Religious worship is a private right and even a communal necessity. Religious experience in its primary form is necessarily sectarian and to establish by law one sect is to threaten the existence of all others. Hence no legal establishment of one set of rites and clergy is to be permitted. Furthermore, by protecting religious sects while denying them official status, religious differences would be prevented from becoming economic and political differences.

Yet it is hard to believe that the drafters of our Constitution did not have in mind the civilizing and unifying force of religion when its meaning, although growing out of ritual and creed, becomes subtilized and universalized by reflection, that is, by religious education. That religions remain plural in their rites and creeds, yet suffuse all of life with a unified meaning was perhaps the hope of the Founding Fathers and perhaps can still be the goal of religious education.

Teaching Machines

When the teaching machine was introduced by S. L. Pressey and B. F. Skinner some time ago, it was a cloud no bigger than a man's hand on the educational horizon. Today it is a sizable cloud indeed. Experience with tape recorders, computers of all sorts, and general sophistication about the ways of a man and a machine promise a revolution in formal schooling.

Calm and judicious pedagogical voices dismiss the development as merely another adjunct to human teaching. They reassure the teacher that he or she will never be replaced (much as horse dealers were once assured that horses would never be replaced by motor cars). This reassurance is justified but it would be surprising indeed if the role of the teacher, like that of the horse, will ever be the same again.

For those who are not familiar with teaching machines, it need only be said that they are devices that by means of a tape or other contrivance present a task to the pupil. The task can be a problem in arithmetic, a word to be spelled, a choice among three or four forms of a sentence, the completion of a map.

Indeed, the variety of learning tasks is almost unlimited—provided only that there is a right answer. Usually in these machines the right answer is followed by a new task; the wrong answer keeps the pupil at the old task or directs him to finding out where he went wrong. The subtlety of the machine is not to be underestimated. Suppose the task is spelling. A machine might ask for the spelling of "deceive," "receive," and "conceive," and then pop in "believe." Or if the task is arithmetic, problems can be varied almost endlessly by a careful program designer so that every variety of fraction, percentage, and number combination is represented by a task.

Furthermore, the reinforcement or reward need not be confined to the prosaic: "That is correct, proceed to the next problem." For the young a comic book, a lollipop, or a brace of tickets to the movies could be served up at strategic moments, and no less ingenious rewards and punishments could easily be contrived for the more mature learners as well.

In other words, those who are muttering about the mechanical nature of the teaching machine are wasting their breath. It is mechanical, but not so stupid nor so rigid as the mutterers would like to believe. On the contrary, being a machine, it is thorough and uniform in its demands, rewards, punishments, and other ministrations. In short, when it works, it is extraordinarily efficient, something most human beings, including teachers, are not.

Oddly enough, the great vulnerability of teaching by machine, as one educator recently pointed out, is that, being machines, they will not work a good deal of the time. The out-of-order sign will always be on a fair proportion of them at any given moment, and teachers will have to become adept at the repair and maintenance of machines, just as they have been forced to become wise in the ways of tape recorders and movie projectors. Skilled technicians being scarce and highly paid, one wonders whether this trend may not solve the economic problem of teachers. By allowing them to retain their title as teachers and changing their function to that of mechanics, our society can have its cake and eat it too. By making teachers do the work of mechanics our citizens can, in all good conscience, pay them the wages of mechanics—something they feel they cannot do so long as teachers are merely instructors.

Properly used, the machines represent a liberation of the teachers, much as the mechanical marvels in agriculture have liberated farmers from drudgery and unproductive toil. If teachers do not readily apprehend this, it is, I believe, because they have conceived of teaching exclusively in terms of one phase of instruction. Seeing this phase of their work threatened by the encroachment of the machine, they are understandably perturbed, just as linotype operators are justifiably perturbed by machines that will make them dispensable.

If this phase of teaching is all there is to it, then one must say to teachers what one says to linotypists and other machine operators about to be displaced by labor-saving devices: "Friends, you are the victims of progress. Some of you will be absorbed in the new order of things. Others are doomed to suffer, but in the long run more people will be employed, more good will be produced, and more happiness will be distributed to more people. In the meantime, let us pass laws to alleviate your distress." Or to put it bluntly, if teaching is what a machine can do better than teachers are now doing, then the machine ought to be doing it.

There are, however, many facets to teaching. Practicing the right response or practicing the finding of the right response is only one facet—the one that is most adaptable to machines. But there is also the facet we call insight or understanding, and there is the facet we might call appreciation. For centuries good teachers have complained that all their time was used up in drill and practice. Suppose now they are freed by the machine to devote themselves to the understanding and appreciation phases of teaching. Will they rejoice at this opportunity or will they perhaps be frightened at having to do something other than perfecting their pupils in the right responses?

I suspect that this is too superficial a solution. Machines for drill, human teachers for insights and appreciation, sounds like a plausible division of labor, but are we so certain that machines cannot manage the other facets also?

What of the movement now well under way with generous impetus from Foundations to stage "educational spectaculars," so to speak? For example, what about the courses in physics in the grand manner that television has been exhibiting to a nation-wide class at early hours of the morning? Cannot the student get his insights from this type of machine teaching? And would this not solve the problems of schools that cannot afford to build laboratories with high-grade equipment nor to hire topflight professors? The television presentation, on the other hand, spares no expense in the way of equipment, professors, assistants, planning, and whatever else it takes to explain and demonstrate the principles of physics.

Surely insight can be promoted in this way simultaneously for millions of viewers. And once the moment of insight has been achieved, supplementary practice on the problems and exercises could be programmed for machine teaching. All we would then need is the machine-tender teacher, the television-operator teacher, and the IBM test grader.

I repeat that those who shrink from these possibilities had better steel themselves to the realities they portend. Large-scale high school and college instruction may be impossible without machine duplication of a relatively small number of teaching performances. And does it matter really whether the pupil gets his principles of physics and chemistry, his mathematics and history, from a television lecturer or from a lecturer standing in the front of the room or hall?

To be sure, the possible ego damage to the local teacher or professor is fearful to contemplate. For the local instructor has to admit that he cannot give a first-rate lesson. High school teachers are more likely to be persuaded of this than college professors, so that unless the professors are themselves to be permitted to perform on television, the venture is in for rough sailing. Something similar to the disinclination of college professors to use textbooks they did not write may well set in. The planners of educational television had better look to their human relations experts before they prescribe it as a panacea for the college enrollment explosion.

Then is nothing educational safe from the machine, from the IBM punch card, and from the electronic brains? In principle, nothing. Anything that can be shown, played, or sung—literature, art, science—all can be adapted for machine duplication and perhaps presented better and certainly more elaborately than the average local schoolroom and teacher can do it.

In practice, however, it is hard to imagine a conversation between a machine and a pupil; it is difficult to imagine the machine and the learner growing together, interacting with each other so that the experience of each changes irreversibly with each moment of instruction. It is even more difficult to conceive of a machine toward which the pupil feels respect and from which he expects understanding and respect. It is difficult to imagine how a machine could, without a word, pass a judgment on a pupil that the pupil will feel more keenly than the most detailed of reports from the battery of tests that the electronic counselors can emit on a second's notice.

Whatever accrues from such conversation cannot be achieved by machines. When teacher and pupil are both part of a unified quest toward something higher than either of them, to use a notion of Froebel's, we are out of the realm of the machine. Particularly when the learning is an insight into values, does the machine have a hard time of it.

Consider, for example, the problem of instilling in a pupil a love of truth or of justice or of freedom. It is not difficult to make a film or to turn out literary materials containing the appropriate sentiments. And perhaps photogenic professors with a gift for the theatrical can, with the help of a Foundation grant, turn out a spectacular that will cause students to surge into streets hungering after justice and freedom. This type of teaching can arouse emotion and incite action. It does not, however, institute a relation between the teacher and pupil such that the meanings of truth and justice and freedom are sharpened by dialectic and honed by conversation. One must be able to talk back to Socrates.

The machine cannot serve the pupil as a life model which interacts with him as his friends do, as do a hero and his worshipers, as do the master and the disciple.

It is of some significance that we do not remember our great teachers as efficient teaching machines, but rather as personalities who literally "personified" for us something that we either valued at the time or came to value in later years. I am sure, to take a personal example, that there were many professors of philosophy who could have lectured as ably and clearly as did the late Edgar Sheffield Brightman at Boston University. Even his own special insights into philosophical doctrines could be gleaned from his writings. Possibly television could convey the eager preoccupation with truth by a religiously and morally committed man. But what device could substitute for his dialogue with students in the class, in interviews, in conferences—some of them conducted in a taxi-cab on the way to lunch in a Chinese restaurant? How can we mechanize the heady sweetness of his praise for a sharp question or a good term paper? How could he, from a television screen, correct your impulsive comment, hasty generalization? How could he via television make you feel mature simply by taking what you said seriously enough to be mercilessly frank about it?

All of this comes to what? Being a highly individualized teacher, Professor Brightman contributed something unique to the learning situation he created. If this contribution was good, the loss of it is not reparable by substituting another teacher through television, tape, or anything or anyone else. It is one thing to put a Brightman *on* television; it is another to remove him from the classroom *by* television. Those who are enthusiastic about the potentialities of putting first-rate teachers on television or into some other form of teaching machine should not forget the possible irreparable loss they may occasion by removing first-rate teachers from the educational scene. Genuine individuals are not comparable and therefore not substitutable.

If a teacher is a source of non-standardized insights; if the teacher is creative enough to produce a highly personal reaction to the world and to the subjects he teaches, then he is a valuable asset and not a machine at all. If he is an inciter to thought; if he can engage in enlightening dialogue; if he enacts a life style that persuades as it reveals, then it is not a teaching machine we are talking about. In this sense there is no more point in talking about any one type of "good" teacher than there is to talk about any one type of "good" artist or "good" personality. The goodness lies in their willingness, indeed, their inability to refrain from interacting with the young in an educative way, and this they do in as many ways as there are individual patterns in their respective lives.

Great and wonderful is the institution that attracts to its faculty a variety of personalities who exemplify the diverse patterns of the good life and who, by teaching, conduct their pupils on their own individual guided tour in the wisdom of the race. In such an institution each classroom is a new perspective from which the world looks new and fresh and revelatory. Great and wonderful are the years one is privileged to spend exploring the world in the company of such teachers. The pressure of life's business makes these years tragically few.

The advent of a teaching machine that can drill the learner with marvelous efficiency and has mechanical means of duplicating a lesson a millionfold through the miracles of electronics only serves to make us ask anew: Just what is teaching and what are teachers for? The answer is at once disturbingly old and suggestively new. Why, teachers teach *themselves*. They themselves are the only subject matter that they alone can teach.

The Other Excuses of Beauty

The American public school from time to time is accused of a shameful neglect of the aesthetic side of education. Teachers of the arts, naturally enough, are most sensitive to the meagerness of budget and stinginess with curricular time that lower the status of their work on the academic totem pole.

Inasmuch as general statements about the American public school, including this one, are probably false, the accusation should be taken to mean that, by and large, on the whole, and ignoring some honorable exceptions, the school works at the arts if time and money remain over from reading, writing, arithmetic, and other intellectual pursuits. Music and the visual arts are rarely required in high schools, and even in the elementary school how much is done and of what quality depends on the individual teacher. It goes without saying that teachers who cannot maneuver easily among the arts are not eager to teach them. Literature is an important exception when it is taught for its aesthetic values, which is itself something exceptional.

It is customary to blame this state of affairs on the fact that the American culture is technological and materialistic. Americans, we are told, have only recently conquered the frontier and have been too busy subduing and controlling nature to be concerned with the finer things in life. In the fight for life, it is argued, efficiency comes before appearance, the applied arts before the fine ones.

Only the American woman, we are told, saved our culture from the brutality and callousness that its men were forced to practice in order to survive and win the new continent. The woman's touch brought flowers into the rude log cabin, and her remembrance of Old World amenities made her crave pretty dresses and school learning for the children amid the hardships and perils of frontier life. Even today the American woman is pictured as dragging the husband to recitals, lectures, and operas when, left to his preferences, he would be content to view in hypnotized absorption a football game or a western on television.

While this may be an outworn stereotype, it has enough validity not to be dismissed, and it has some importance in trying to discover the reasons for the neglect of aesthetic education in our schools. The stereotype helps to explain the indifference of the American public to the fine arts, especially the avant-garde fine arts. It is not so helpful in explaining the role of aesthetic experience in the life of the common man.

In weaving the fabric of daily life aesthetic considerations are pervasive and important. The most primitive guide to action is the appearance of things and persons. The way the sky looks, the way a voice sounds, the way a cliff threatens and a lake invites, not to speak of the way a human body is shaped and colored, are our first clues as to whether we shall be attracted to these objects or be repelled by them. In what other way could man have learned that a dark sky threatens hunting expeditions and a dark sea may eventuate in destructive waves? In the beginning, man had to judge the character of men and things by their appearance and to this day he cannot reconcile beauty with evil, notwithstanding all experience with divorce courts, mirages, and advertising.

That appearances are not always safe guides to action was the hard lesson that man had to learn and relearn. Far from being indifferent to appearances, the common man is their most abject slave. He is gullible because he trusts what appeals to his senses; and because he is so trusting, it pays for advertisers to create appearances that will beguile him away from questions of efficiency, utility, and price. It is not the rude, untutored man who is indifferent to the surface qualities of objects, but the trained man who looks for less superficial clues.

The development of science can be thought of as the displacement of aesthetic clues to action by other and more reliable ones. The weather bureau is, one hopes, more to be relied upon about tomorrow's weather than the appearance of the sky at eventide; chemical analysis is a far safer guide to the nutritional properties of foods than their appearance. So as sciences advance, appearances become less and less useful as a clue to the nature of things or their potentialities for human life.

And yet after all this is admitted, an astonishing amount of our conduct is based on aesthetic impressions. A poorly modulated voice and awkward expression lead us to infer a poorly cultivated man. On our first meeting with a man we make judgments about his personality and character on the basis of his appearance, gestures, and general demeanor. Even in medicine, the appearance of the patient, the general impression of toxicity or good health are the first clues to more refined analysis. Psychiatrists, one can be sure, also depend on how the patient looks, the sound of his voice, the phrasing of his speech, gestures, and posture for clues to deeper diagnosis.

In our work we carry about an image of normality regarding the objects with which we are dealing. The plumber knows how a properly constructed joint should appear; the mechanic trusts his ear for the proper tuning of a motor; the athletic coach watches the form of his athletes; and there is a tradition that women are unusually shrewd at interpreting small aesthetic cues and that their husbands are not very good at it. The orator senses rapport with his audience; the salesman relies on aesthetic cues to tell him when to move in for the closing of the deal. The appearance of houses and clothing prompt us to conjecture about the sort of people to whom they belong. Finally, who can define charm? Who can itemize that rare syndrome of aesthetic clues that makes a person irresistible to everyone? Who can help the young lady who, although possessing all of the qualities commonly needed for popularity, nevertheless does not enjoy it?

Some day, perhaps, all such cues will be displaced by more scientifically determined signs, more reliable signs. With battalions of doctoral candidates in psychology and sociology ready to seek significant correlations, and electronic computers available to speed the quest, we can expect to rely less and less on the appearance of things for knowledge about them.

For the time being, however, aesthetic clues are still widely used, and it is important that appearances deceive as little as possible. For example, our personal appearance should tell the truth about us. Our neckties should not pronounce us gay blades if at bottom we are conservative fellows. Our neatly trimmed hedges and lawns should not tell the world that we are conformists if, at heart and in truth, we crave undisciplined rock gardens. It is useless to admonish people not to judge by appearance; they will persist in doing so, rarely investigating us sufficiently well to find the reality behind the appearance.

If we lay claim to authentic individuality, our appearance should not belie it; our speech should not deceive the listener. Weird appearance for the sake of novelty gives the impression of the bizarre or the eccentric. Careless conformity to the mode in speech, dress, as well as in thought, proclaims a conformity of spirit. Part of the art of life is to fashion a set of externals that invites the interest of the beholder to the reality within and does not disappoint or deceive when the invitation is accepted.

That our people are not so enthusiastic about art galleries and symphony concerts as one might wish is deplorable. We shall come to this a bit later, but in deploring this, we tend to overlook the fact that for sheer volume of aesthetic satisfaction and revulsion the objects we encounter every day bulk larger than all the museums and concert halls put together.

One wonders, for example, how our immediate ancestors managed to construct such horrible buildings on their main streets in the late years of the last century and the early years of this one. The ugly one-story garage type of building, the square boxes with a feeble attempt at a false brick front, anything in fact, that would house a shop or a store have made riding through these villages a depressing experience. Does such ugliness express the values of their builders? In this connection it is worth noting how often the impression one forms about the caliber and character of a business firm is based on the type of lettering, the size, the colors used in its sign. One does not look for bargains in a restaurant or shop whose sign is lettered in neat black script on a clear white or gold background; and if the sign is huge and bright, one is suspicious of the prices asked for the merchandise displayed within, however low they may be.

The graceful posture, the pleasant voice, the careful speech on which the Athenians placed so much stress were supposed to express a harmony of character within. The outward signs, it is true, did not create inward grace, although Plato sometimes speaks as if he thought they could. Our own times have denigrated the value of externals, possibly on the ground that they were not so important as the inner reality, and one is led to infer that we are dealing here with rough diamonds whose worth is not expressed by their polish and setting. But uncut diamonds and unexpressed virtue are diamonds and virtue only potentially; until they are expressed, they operate as neither diamonds nor virtue. One might hope, therefore, that our tastemakers, our schools, our leaders of opinion might support a campaign for authenticity—not merely for originality or non-conformity, or the courage to be different, or bohemianism, but for honest self-manifestation in one's clothing, speech, house, garden, and street.

There is another set of observations that gives the lie to the contention that Americans are indifferent to the aesthetic values. Aside from the semi-conscious use of the surface qualities of things as clues to their character, we use the arts whenever we wish to enhance the importance of some life activity. Music and decorations are considered essential to weddings, funerals, commencements, banquets, and sport spectacles. We emphasize the importance of events by formalizing them, by giving them aesthetic properties that express the nature or mood of the occasion. Candlelight, fine napery, and silver set the mood for a dinner party. Certain types of music are supposed to be peculiarly appropriate to intimate dinners *à deux,* certain others to armies on parade.

So ubiquitous is this ceremonial and celebrative use of the arts that some historians are tempted to find in it the origin of the arts. Indeed, it is a powerful means of social control because the ritualized behavior invoked for important social occasions keeps the appropriate feelings on tap for these occasions. A culture that has lost its sense of importance, or is no longer sure as to what is important, finds itself with no aesthetic models wherewith to condition the young. It is perhaps a sign of our difficulty in generating appropriate emotional responses to democracy that we have never ceremonialized the acts of voting or collective deliberation and decision. The young go on the principle that if these activities were important, they would have been ceremonialized in song, story, and pageantry, as are the world series and football games.

Finally, one must point to the undeniable fact that even the untutored person spontaneously responds to the beautiful, or to what he regards as beautiful. The appearance of things is not a matter of indifference in daily life; only overwhelming considerations of utility completely push it out of the way. But given half a chance, the consumer will pay a bit extra for appearance in his possessions. He seeks a beautiful landscape and a beautiful mate. He listens to music, decorates tools and weapons as well as his house. He buys decorations if he cannot make them. The hunger for beauty is as real as the hunger for comfort, companionship, and truth. There are many aesthetic theories that purport to explain this craving. These one may question, but not the fact behind them.

If, then, it is true that all men use the aesthetic qualities of things as clues, as means of underlining their other values, and for their own sake as well, why do we complain that the aesthetic dimension of education and, presumably, of life is given shabby treatment in our culture?

The truth of the matter would seem to be that the level at which the aesthetic factors in life are utilized are not so high as the critics think they ought to be. And how high ought they to be? Once more there are many, many theories of what makes aesthetic objects aesthetically or artistically excellent, but for the moment we can pass them by. In any period the working standard of aesthetic experience is represented by the taste and judgment of the man who has studied and reflected on a wide variety of artistic objects: by the enlightened critic and the connoisseur.

Just as good physics is what students of physics say it is, and good housebuilding is what the competent architect says it is, so good music is what the student of music says it is. If students disagree, they disagree, but their right to dispute does not give license to the ignorant man to substitute his own standard.

When we compare the kinds of music and art and poetry and drama that the average man chooses with the kinds the connoisseur approves, the discrepancy is impressive, and it is this discrepancy that disturbs the art educator. It is the indifference of the common man to the fine arts and to the approved exemplars of them that causes the complaint.

Matters would not be so bad if one could demonstrate that our people yearned for the fine arts but were deprived of access to them by lack of money, opportunity, or the selfishness of some aristocracy. But there is no great yearning that need remain unsatisfied or frustrated. Nowhere, at any time, have the opportunities to experience serious music, art, and drama been so numerous as they now are through the media of television, movie, magazine, and phonograph. All who want these things can manage to get them even in the desert and wilderness. That they are not displayed more often through the mass media is due to the fact —the managers of these media say—that the people do not want them in sufficient numbers to make them attractive to advertising sponsors.

If the people do not yearn for the fine arts, it is not because they are inaccessible but because they are satisfied with popular forms of the arts. They are art-sated, not art-hungry. Radio has become little more than a public jukebox for popular music; magazines and house furnishings supply visual art to the home; and television furnishes a steady fare of drama that is eminently satisfying to millions upon millions of citizens. The genius of mass production has made available at low cost a plenitude of music, art, drama, and entertainment that the majority likes. Who could ask for anything more?

The American public school is therefore put in an awkward position vis-à-vis the arts. It cannot very well raise the alarm that the people will be deprived of aesthetic experience and satisfactions if art education is not provided for the young. On the contrary, the young are already enjoying a rather fulsome aesthetic experience. As for the enjoyment of the fine arts, just what, the cautious school board member might ask, is endangered by not appreciating them? He could point out that we manage to turn out enough professional performers for our needs. For those who would like to become enthusiastic amateurs there are ample opportunities for taking elective courses in high school and college, or for securing private tuition. No one who really wants a musical or artistic education is being denied one. As for the rest, what purpose would be served by cramming down their throats expensive instruction in art that they neither want nor need?

Unfortunately, the answer to these objections is neither short nor simple, and I am not at all sure that it can be phrased so as to convince the school board member who raises these objections in good faith, that is, who really believes them himself.

One might retort that schools are almost never guided by what the pupils say they need or even what they will probably need in adult life. For one thing, what a person needs in the way of schooling depends on the level of life he hopes to lead. Since the average expectation is not very high, the amount of schooling needed for life outside one's vocational specialty is relatively small and perhaps getting smaller. Machines do much of our reading, calculating, and thinking for us, and a man who cannot read has far more access to information than his counterpart had, let us say, in 1860. Mass production reduces the amount of knowledge and skill needed to utilize its product. Ready-mixed cakes render the skill of cake baking otiose; washing machines and other appliances have stripped housekeeping of what little dignity it once had; but who would not exchange the dignity for the convenience?

Only when one is dissatisfied with the average level of life does he need more than average schooling. Only when there is dissatisfaction with the mass-produced article, ideas, and taste, is more than a minimal amount of schooling necessary. If a school purveys and extols examples of science and art that differ from the ideas and tastes that are current, it becomes a critic of its time and values. In doing this the school engenders dissatisfaction. Two kinds of science and art act as accusers of the common knowledge and taste: the classics, or the examples of excellence from the past, and the experimental, frontier activities of the cultural avant-garde in science, art, and every other area of human life. The school is more likely to confront the present with its past glories than with its future possibilities, but even so it is still far from rubber-stamping popular ideas and taste.

The purpose of art education in public school, if taken seriously, must be to change the taste of the untutored consumer, and to do this it has to make him dissatisfied with what he and his esteemed friends are now enjoying without any sense of deprivation.

Unfortunately, the fine arts represent "difficult beauty," and one has to acquire a taste for them by training and discipline. Hence to ask the happy adolescent not only to reject what his world salutes as successful, but to undergo hard hours of study to become receptive to another sort of aesthetic pleasure is asking a good deal. The demand is unconvincing because failure to meet it does not jeopardize vocational success or, for that matter, any other kind that he values. Educators who in one breath argue that the curriculum should be shaped by the felt needs of the student or the social order of his time cannot in the same breath urge the expenditure of time and money for a type of training of which neither the student nor the social order feels any demonstrable need.

Two alternatives are open to the school: either announcing boldly that it is concerned not primarily with current needs of the social order but with what a high order of human excellence entails for education, or waiting patiently for the logic of events to work itself out. The first alternative is taken by schools, colleges, and universities that by tradition and endowment can afford to ignore political pressures. One wonders, for example, what the history of Harvard and Phillips Exeter Academy would have been, had they been dependent for their support on the state legislature or the municipal authorities. These and similar institutions have been able to present a model of aspiration and life that has remained fairly stable in its fundamental values throughout many social changes and in the face of powerful social pressures. Such steadfastness is not a moral obligation for the public school because the impossible, to paraphrase Kant, cannot be a moral imperative.

The other alternative—waiting for the logic of events to work itself out—is beyond the power of any school to control. School people can, however, by being aware of the trends capitalize on them. Paradoxically, mass production both depends on conformity and is at the same time its greatest enemy. It depends on it because in mass production large numbers of consumers must be satisfied with uniform objects. There can be only so many different models before the unit cost of the mass-produced article is threatened. On the other hand, mass production also depends on rapid change of models. Whether the obsolescence is built in or not, the public must be induced to get tired of the old article. Variety, therefore, competes with uniformity in the battle of mass production.

Because with modern methods of production the efficiency and utility of competing automobiles, refrigerators, toasters, and television sets tend to become equalized, the appearance of the article takes on a decisive importance. Novelty achieves a premium, and novelty is provided only by creative minds. Just as novelty in contrivance is a product of inventive genius, so novelty of appearance is a product of artistic creativity. The fine arts and their practitioners are the seedbed of creativity and novelty with respect to the perceptual qualities of things. So it begins to look as if a technological society depending for its life on large-scale mass production may be saved by the creativity in the fine arts, which are, on the face of it, the very antithesis of mass production.

Sooner or later a people in whom artistic creativity is killed off will lose the impetus to novelty that gives to their industrial products a style and charm making them attractive on the competitive market. From a people in whom aesthetic activity and taste is dead there cannot emerge the group of artistic performers and creators whose work keeps the aesthetic kettle stirring and bubbling. An avant-garde is the price of vitality not only in the arts themselves but in the whole complex of mass production. Mass culture has to tolerate small groups of experimenters who gamble with the future and risk the scorn of their contemporaries. The seers and prophets of old have their counterparts today in the eccentric souls who are compelled (for no sane and sober burgher could undertake it voluntarily) to see what others do not, hear what escapes the ears of the multitude, create forms of feeling and thought that seem alien and disconnected with what is familiar and intelligible.

For the arts are both the prologues and the epitaphs of the social order. Like antennae, they discern early in the game the rumblings of the future and shape of things to come. Sometimes even the artist does not understand what his own shorthand of form, color, and sound means. Sometimes it turns out that the artist has not sensed the future at all, but rather discerned the meaning of his own time in a way that others did not. Perhaps what becomes classic in art as the epochs roll on are precisely those masterpieces that captured the peculiar flavor of an era that was ending.

But prologue or epitaph, avant-garde or classic, serious art is inaccessible to the untrained. If a step beyond popular art is necessary, then aesthetic education is necessary to take that step, and the school is the logical place to take it.

Once training in the arts is shown to be essential to mass-production culture, beauty will have an excuse other than itself. That it will enhance the aesthetic enjoyment of the learner is sufficient justification for aesthetic education for the individual, but not for a school system.

Nevertheless, keeping the mass production system vigorous by aesthetic education will inevitably have other effects as well. One of these might be the desire for authentic self-manifestation. And it is inconceivable that once the form of manifestation is brought to self-consciousness the content will escape scrutiny. To ask seriously which clothes, speech, posture, yards, and buildings express our real character is to ask what that real character is. The attempt to externalize our inner life perforce discloses some of the elements that resist integration; it reveals all the awkwardness and disproportions of the spirit. The escape from self-revelation, when revelation would be embarrassing, is afforded to us by masks. Conventionalized speech, dress, and demeanor are such masks. When we all don the same mask, we become, for all practical purposes, faceless, and faceless, for some reason, we do not want to be.

There is this to be said for the Hegelians, however much one may tire of their long-winded dialectics: the inner is not complete until made outer. To be is not to be perceived, or to be thought, or to be felt merely; to be is to act oneself out, to become a vector in the flow of reality, and this the inner, as inner, cannot accomplish. The aesthetic quality of our outer acts is a barometer, a sign, if you like, of what we are and how matters stand with us.

It is not, then, that the American people despise or have no time for the aesthetic dimension of life. We can no more avoid using aesthetic cues to life, can no more avoid enhancing our values by aesthetic devices, can no more avoid seeking the beautiful, than we can avoid breathing.

But in every age the level at which this aesthetic life is lived can vary from the conventional, habitual, and easy, to the creative and the difficult. The former level, represented in our time by the popular mass-produced arts and crafts, requires no formal training in aesthetic activity; the latter does. It is the role of the fine arts in the school and in the social order that is the crux of the problem, and to this the school can now turn with a degree of hope and confidence that strangely enough is being supplied by the demands of a technological society working out its own inner logic.

Planning for Excellence

The most revolutionary educational proposal of the twentieth century was that the school and all its personnel, from pupils to administrators, be committed to the method of intelligence. It was a radical proposal because heretofore schools had been committed to imparting a selected set of learning skills and a store of information wherewith, if all went well, children were to behave intelligently when they achieved adulthood. It was not expected that the pupils would exercise the method of intelligence *during* the process of acquiring skill and knowledge.

Being intelligent, according to the new doctrine, was not the same as being bright or sensible. Intelligence was identified as the experimental (scientific) search for highly probable means to critically appraised and deliberately chosen goals. The method of intelligence became equated with problem-solving. The school, if it were to be committed to the method of intelligence, had to display all the characteristics of an intelligent person: the ability of stating and appraising goals, seeking and testing means, which, as it turns out, are also the characteristics of planning. Thus the meanings of problem-solving, intelligent behavior, and planning converged on equivalence.

To a large extent the history of public schooling in America during the first half of the current century will have to be written in terms of the acceptance or rejection of this doctrine. The result of intensive research and argumentation to date does not justify a clear acceptance or rejection. Undoubtedly, children do learn by solving problems, and what they so learn they learn well and painlessly. Whether or not they learn the conceptual structures which constitute science, mathematics, or history as by-products of problem-solving depends a good deal on which problems are chosen for study. That children master these subjects or disciplines as a by-product of extricating themselves from real-life predicaments is doubtful. The fortunes of planning in education ebb and flow as problem-solving or the method of intelligence is accepted or rejected as a design for schooling.

The curriculum, naturally enough, was the first target for planning. The traditional curriculum was not intelligent, it was argued, because it was not the result of planning. Such modifications as it had undergone were forced upon it by all sorts of *ad hoc* pressures. The need for clerks and bookkeepers, for example, put a premium on arithmetic and handwriting. Textile manufacture helped introduce drawing, and multitudes of immigrants frightened the school authorities into putting more emphasis on instruction that would assimilate them into the American way of life. The school was to be America's protection against mobocracy. Science met stiff resistance from curriculum makers until the nation's economy put a high value on the agricultural and mechanical arts. In short, the curriculum had grown more or less vigorously in many directions by reacting to a variety of social imperatives.

The arguments for a deliberately planned curriculum were of three sorts. First, planning, being an exercise of intelligence, would align the curriculum more closely to deliberately chosen objectives. Planning would clear away deadwood, historical accretions of no functional value, prejudices, and accidents of tradition. It was another way of cutting loose from the dominance of the past and the values of the upper-middle class. The demise of Greek and Latin symbolized the new freedom.

Second, if learners, teachers, and citizens planned the curriculum together, the acceptance of the curriculum would be automatic and complete; the planners could not reject the work of their own hands, so to speak. Much of the young learner's traditional resistance to the benefits of schooling was allegedly caused by his inability to understand the usefulness of certain school tasks, and such reinforcement as his parents provided for his discontent was held to be due to similar misunderstandings.

Third, the act of planning would itself be a training in intelligence. Pupils, faculty, and citizens would in the course of curriculum planning come to formulate problems, gather and evaluate data, project and test hypotheses. Indeed, by some advocates of planning this was thought to be its most important and distinctive outcome.

In addition to these arguments in behalf of curriculum planning, it was obvious that it was or could be a democratic way of conducting education. Thus it was thought appropriate for all those participating in the activities of the school to have a voice both in setting up its goals and selecting the means. Inasmuch as everyone, save perhaps outlaws, had a stake in and a concern for the outcomes of the educative process, the literal application of the principle made for a large planning group indeed. Nevertheless, the more stern and unflinching advocates of this view did not shrink from this consequence and encouraged parents, citizen groups from labor, industry, business, and farmers, to become involved in the planning process. The walls of the school were to come tumbling down, ending what was held to be an artificial separation between school and community.

Community planning had its counterpart in classroom planning with pupils and teachers as participants. Goals as well as means were to come under scrutiny, for goals were to be geared to the conditions of the times, but these being as changeable as water, could never be fixed. There were no eternal truths to provide a fixed content of the curriculum. For example, a widely exhibited educational film shows how a course in United States history begins with the class listing the outcomes to be sought from the course and voting as to which should be adopted as goals for the class. Neither the teacher nor the textbook was regarded as an authority on the objectives of United States history study. The "felt" importance of the various topics as determined by a vote of the students was decisive for structuring the course, but one gets the impression from the instructor's smiling face that the students' choice coincided with his own. The film goes on to teach the lesson that this planning not only made the study of history more meaningful to the students, but that it also provided practice in the use of intelligence and helped to form attitudes appropriate to democratic group action.

This trend in educational thought with its stress on intelligence, democracy, and planning coincided with a strong interest of educational philosophers in using the schools as an agency of social reform. George Counts' *Dare the School Build a New Social Order?* and the articles in *The Social Frontier* were typical of this movement. With depression, dictatorships, and war on the scene, it was natural for educators as well as social theorists to look to planning or the method of intelligence as a source of salvation. Given intelligent participation by all interested parties, such societal predicaments as taxes and poverty and such personal problems as choosing a mate or vocation were bound to have a prosperous issue.

Excellence in this scheme of education was not conceived primarily as the attainment by individuals of an exceptionally high order of cognitive or artistic achievement. Excellence was located instead in the quality of the society itself. The more sharable the experience, John Dewey argued, the better the social order, and intelligent coping with life's exigencies was precisely what made it more sharable. Accordingly, the educator's heart was warmed not so much by an impressive display of memory, thoroughness of reading, writing, and computing skill, or even by acute reasoning, that is, by scholastic virtuosity, as by the democratic functioning of a group in confrontation with a real predicament.

So during the Thirties, Forties, and early Fifties our leading educational theorists argued that general education was education for democracy and that to achieve it the school should institutionalize the method of intelligence in life, notably by planning of all kinds. Education, in short, was conceived as democracy in action.

Since the Sputnik ascent, however, planning, education for life adjustment, democracy, and citizenship have become sneer words to hurl at the Progressive educationists. Indeed, things have come to such a pass that the mere utterance of these words makes argument unnecessary; to some minds they carry their own condemnation, like "wife beater" or "Communist."

If one disengages the sense from the nonsense, one finds that the rejection of planning is not equivalent to the acceptance of an unplanned school. It does, however, make a shambles of the argument that curriculum planning by teachers and pupils is to be regarded as part of the educative process. It could be defended as long as practice in intelligent behavior, rather than systematic knowledge, was regarded as the *prime* outcome of schooling. One could then exercise the method of intelligence by collectively deliberating on what project should be undertaken, how the task was to be divided, and how it should be approached.

However, once considerations of national defense, national pride, and international politics gave priority to learning certain subjects—science, mathematics, and language—there was not much point in deliberating about what should be taught or learned. One does not plan what is already commanded.

It is a mistake to believe that these commands were issued only because of Sputnik. To tell the truth, they had been issued quietly but firmly when the industrial revolution emerged as the triumphant way of life of the West and of the world. Sputnik's beeps merely made them more audible. Sooner or later a technological civilization had to convert all forms of power to technological power. Political power, military power, persuasive power—all were destined to become abjectly dependent on science and technology. Sputnik was a dramatic way of announcing to the world that this destiny had at last been fulfilled.

In this crisis two indictments were made against the American high school. First, that its college preparatory course was insufficiently rigorous as compared to Russian and Continental programs, and second, that not enough young people were studying science, mathematics, and foreign languages to enable us to compete favorably in all the military and political facets of the Cold War. These defects were blamed upon the educationists who, it was argued, had planned away hard subjects in favor of easy ones and rigorous intellectual discipline in favor of life-adjustment activities.

From college presidents and professors, from A.B. degree holders who had been forced to take courses in education in order to obtain a teaching certificate, from newspaper editors, industrialists, and, indeed, from men in all sorts of high places, came a blistering attack on the educationists. The criticism is a rich broth of resentment against economic and political theories, against the political maneuvers of some public school officials, against teachers colleges and colleges of education, and against certain theories of child rearing. The furor was not without its comic relief, provided by tilts with windmills, denunciation of imaginary villains, and much straining at gnats while swallowing camels.

It is very difficult to weigh these indictments. One can quote statistics to prove or disprove almost any assertion about the American schools. The more important point is that the professional educators did not respond to the crisis with unity, conviction, or imagination. That they failed to do so, I believe, was due to the fact that they seriously misconstrued the educational demands implicit in the social order; that if they thought at all about these demands, it was in terms of an order that had quietly slipped into history. They responded to the charges with statistical defenses, pleas of poverty, and counteraccusations which had ample truth behind them, but which did not convince the public because they were beside the point.

Scientists, military men, and industrialists took over the leadership in curriculum planning. It was left to James B. Conant, ex-president of Harvard University, an institution not noted for its interest in public schools, to bail out the American high school and to allay the fears of the public and the indignation of the United States Navy's outspoken Admiral H. G. Rickover.

There has been curriculum planning since Sputnik, but it is regarded neither as training in intelligence nor training in democracy. It is planning incited and controlled by government and industry with educators scurrying to find means rather than to choose goals. Military needs and the needs of a technological society have reduced the priorities of the older forms of citizenship education. One wishes that educational leaders had been more sensitive to the changes that were brewing beneath the surface of life, changes that called for modifications in the school formula to provide for democratic citizenship in a technological civilization. I am sure that a careful scanning of the literature will disclose unheard prophets who sounded the alarms and called upon us to change our patterns of economic and political thinking.

But who in the field of education was doing the social analysis and promulgating an education theory based upon it? Who were the vocal and articulate prophets? I think it can be said that the Progressive philosophers of education were. Indeed, an illusion was created that their theories had been translated into practice all over the land, an illusion that rendered so much of the bitter criticism leveled against Progressivism into undeserved tribute or undeserved reproach. The difficulty with the Progressive theory was not that it was false, but rather that it was geared to a social order that had changed its ground rules about the time John Dewey formulated with classical precision its social and educational problems. What I am saying, I suppose, is that John Dewey's *Democracy and Education* was not an adequate guide for modern mass democracy and education.

In highly condensed form, the change can be characterized by noting that education for democracy now entails a high order of knowledge about the world as well as appropriate attitudes toward social problems. It is no longer enough to be *intelligent* about taxation, international trade, nuclear fission, and gross national product, if by intelligent is meant taking a problem-solving, willing-to-be-informed-about, willing-to-discuss-it attitude. One now has to study formally and systematically a good deal of economics, sociology, and physics in order to undertake fruitful problem-solving and discussion. Good citizenship in a modern democracy demands conceptual readiness as well as appropriate attitudes and procedures.

The military men, the industrialists, and the politicians have become explosively aware that intelligence without knowledge and skill is not enough to meet the demands of technology. While beating the educationists over the head with this discovery, the critics of the school system (and its defenders) failed to notice that the educational requirements for citizenship had also changed. The need for scholastic excellence is no longer confined to the occupational elites; it is the *sine qua non* of the new democratic citizenship.

Or to put it another way, the minimum cognitive achievement needed for good citizenship is today nearer to what the graduate of a four-year undergraduate college is presumed to have than to what a high school diploma represents. The spirit of the crackerbarrel, the group discussion, and the town meeting is still a necessity but is no longer sufficient, by itself, for a democratic citizenry.

Granting all this, granting that one cannot think technologically or politically without a high order of cognitive content, the simple truth that gave point to John Dewey's insistence on the method of intelligence still remains to be dealt with. Cognitive content is divided among many domains of knowledge. Much of it is recorded in isolated statements of fact from which the drama of their discovery and the story of their relations have melted out. Although thinking with facts and relations should be part of what we mean by studying a subject, in practice the thinking part gets postponed to later years and work is concentrated on recall of predigested facts, descriptions, and explanations.

Even today, courses in the sciences and indeed in all subjects of study are not wholly free from this charge, although it is now difficult to find many teachers who defend memorization as a primary method of learning. That practice in thinking with the materials of a subject is an important part of learning that subject is acknowledged by the ubiquitous set of problems found at the end of each chapter of the textbook. But that practice in thinking with a variety of cognitive materials is needed in order to structure social problems is by no means obvious. Certainly it is not obvious to the advocates of the theory that, given enough content in separate subjects, political or citizenship thinking will take care of itself. What the emphasis on planning, or what might be called molar problem-solving, did accomplish, namely, to afford practice in thinking collectively about social problems, still has to be provided for somewhere within the school, even though it cannot hope to qualify as a design for the total curriculum.

Excellence in citizenship entails, therefore, not only an upgrading of the cognitive content wherewith to think about social problems, but also a high order of deliberative skill whereby knowledge is selected and used to formulate these problems. Anyone can verify this assertion by trying his hand at formulating the problem of international trade or disarmament. To abandon the cultivation of the art of political thinking is to risk serious consequences. Of these, the most serious is that the doctrine that political decisions should be shaped by the individual intelligent citizen will be reduced to an empty posture. Once these decisions are left to elites, the inner logic of economic systems, or the vagaries of international politics, democracy, new or old, is done for. Yet the planning for excellence in political education is hard to find amid the vigorous plannings for scientific and technological education.

There is, however, an even more basic reason in the light of which the schools should be planning for excellence. I refer to a peculiar paradox of our time, namely, that while living *pretty well* requires relatively little formal schooling, living *really well* calls for an appalling amount of it. The key to the paradox is that to live pretty well one merely has to reap the benefits of mass production: ready-made clothes, cars, entertainment values, and ideas. To live really well is to live as an authentic individual. Individuals, if authentic, cannot make do with mass-produced entertainment values, ideas, and styles of life, however grateful they are for mass-produced cars, television sets, and refrigerators. That so much of our life must be collectivized only emphasizes the difficulties of living as economically, politically, morally, and aesthetically free individuals. Indeed, it is difficult even to bestir ourselves to desire the really good when the pretty good is already so much better than the world has ever known. Of this the young are more aware than their elders.

In the light of these new demands for excellence, the rationale for planning to which leading educational theorists have been committed needs to be re-examined. For one thing, the supposition that the valid educative needs of the pupil are defined by his day-to-day predicaments and that he and his teachers can plan his studies in accordance with their demands becomes doubtful in the face of the massive imperatives of citizenship, national safety, and the problems of authentic individuality in a technological civilization. Planning of projects by students can only take place within a framework of plans already made for them. Thus if studying mathematics is no longer to be a matter of choice, student planning is restricted to devising projects within mathematics. This may still be worth doing but cannot lay claim to genuine autonomy in curriculum planning.

Nor is there much relevance in calling together representatives of labor, business, industry, and sundry civic enterprises to plan what children should be taught in school, unless it is to improve the school's public relations. The logic of events has undercut a curriculum that represents a compromise among group demands. In short, shaping the curriculum is no longer a problem of democratic group dynamics, just as it is no longer a method for practicing the method of intelligence.

All this does not make the educative enterprise an automatic self-regulating instruction factory. There is still a need for planning, albeit of a different sort, for different purposes.

First of all, we shall need a systematic reconstruction of both the content and organization of the subjects of instruction. There is the problem of selecting from an overwhelming array of knowledge those key ideas and relations that are suitable for general education. This is a job that specialists in each field in cooperation with curriculum specialists are just beginning. Let us hope that it will be a cooperation of equals.

Next, there is the problem of pedagogical strategy of how to organize the materials for instruction so as to produce not only knowledge in science and technology, but also the knowledge, attitudes, and appreciations required for excellence in all aspects of life. Let us hope that professional educators can restore and maintain a balance that is now seriously disturbed.

Then there is the matter of organizing instruction to meet the needs not only of the gifted, who are now having some trouble eluding the talent searchers, but also other deviants who make up the fiction called the "average child."

It would be a pity indeed if all the distinctions and refinements of pedagogical method resulting from a half century of study were to be thrown out in favor of a rough-and-ready conviction that one method, one mode of organization, one approach, and one style of teaching will do for everyone. And while it is heartening to witness the glow of discovery in the eyes of liberal arts professors when they stumble on an educational fact or generalization that has been in the educationist textbooks for a score of years, it is a socially wasteful process not to learn from the experience of others.

Finally, there is the staggering task of planning for new levels of aspiration—a desire for excellence not only in rockets and computers but also in the quality of personal and social life—not for the few but for the many.

All of this planning will have to be undertaken in the face of rapidly changing circumstances. Developments in teaching machines, television instruction, and other devices have brought the teaching occupation to the eve of great differentiation. Furthermore, new insights into the teaching-learning process promise to alter the placement and sequences of subject matter and topics within subject matter. All of these and many other developments have been discussed for many years, but the time for their acceptance had to wait for changes that were political and technological rather than educational.

If educational theorists of the Thirties were overly concerned with reconstructing the social order, they were, at least, interested in understanding it and passionately committed to a democratic dream. In latter days neither the interest nor the passion is easy to find in the multitudes of projects, studies, institutes, conferences, and workshops devoted to technical and specialized problems. But in order to plan for excellence in the new social order some educational thinkers will have to emerge from the Platonic Cave, for a while at least. These thinkers will need a sensitivity to social change that in recent decades has been manifested more often by the poet, dramatist, and painter than by the scientist. The artist senses a dislocation in the body politic long before it feels the first twinge of pain; science diagnoses the malady only after the pain has become acute. The planner for excellence must, Janus-like, look in two directions at once: to art for the premonitions of things to come, to science for the means of their control. Art senses the individual, the concrete, the perspective of the person, whereas science by its very nature looks to the general, the universal, the impersonal.

One would like to hope that educators, including educationists, can regain the initiative in this planning for excellence, for it is not a sign of health in a society to have institutions abdicate or lose their primary functions to groups whose primary function is something else. Much as the contributions of President Conant and Admiral Rickover are appreciated by the nation and educational profession, it is the professional educator, the expert in the control of formal learning, upon whom the responsibility for a rational system of schooling rests.

"Planning" is a bad word to social conservatives because it connotes regimentation as against individual freedom. But as Karl Mannheim pointed out, the choice is no longer between planning and not planning, but is the choice of *who* will plan and *what* will be planned. In education, "planning" is also a bad word insofar as it connotes a denial of the importance of logically organized subject matter, mastery of the cognitive skills, and high achievement. But in education, as in economics, there is no choice whether to plan or not to plan. The question is rather who shall do the planning and to what end. The right to plan is his who has labored to acquire the knowledge and courage to look ahead and outwit the times. It is up to the educational profession to demonstrate and exercise this right.

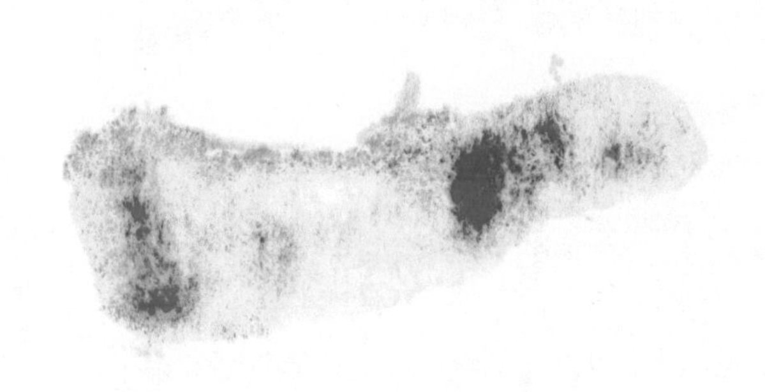

Date Due